*Selling cars will be the highest paying,
easiest work you'll ever do...or selling cars will be
one of the lowest paying, hardest jobs you'll ever have!*

Earn Over

$100,000

Selling Cars

Every Year

*A step-by-step guide to understanding the
potential the car business offers anyone who's
serious about turning pro and earning the big bucks.
And the steps to follow to make it happen.*

*For every salesperson and manager
who wants to become a high achiever.*

Joe Verde

Earn Over

$100,000

Selling Cars

Every Year

Joe Verde

Copyright © 2011 by Joe Verde

ISBN#: 978-1-4507-5568-9

Printed in the United States of America

Inquiries should be addressed to Permissions Department, Joe Verde Sales & Management Training, Inc., 27125 Calle Arroyo, San Juan Capistrano, California 92675-2753.

Joe Verde Training Network®, JVTN®, VSA®, The New Basics™ and Joe Verde® when it relates to automotive industry, are all registered trademarks of Joe Verde, Joe Verde Sales & Management Training, Inc.

This book contains edited chapters from the Joe Verde® books, "How To Sell A Car Today" and "A Dealer's Guide To Recovery & Growth"; plus information from Joe Verde® live class course workbooks and from JVTN®.

joeverde.com • (800) 445-6217 • (949) 489-3780

This book is dedicated to every salesperson who has the guts to work on straight commission.

My goal is to show you how to become that professional in sales your customers need today, so you can sell more cars, have more fun, and definitely make more money.

I also want to thank everyone at Joe Verde Sales & Management Training, Inc., for helping to make our company the #1 training organization in the car business.

– A Note About Results We've Posted In This Book –

We verify and document every results comment we get from salespeople who attend our workshops and train on JVTN®, before we post them. However, we won't be including their full name and the name of their dealership in the comments you'll read in this book.

Why? Here's a request from a salesperson we've congratulated before in print...

"Please take my name off the comment. I don't mind sharing what I've learned and how I sell 30 to 50 units every month. But I'm getting too many calls where it seems like they're more interested in justifying why they can't duplicate what I'm doing instead of trying to do the same, and I need to spend my time selling, thanks!"

That's too bad, but I know he's right because other salespeople have told us the same thing. If we've used your comment in this book, congratulations – you are a high achiever in sales. Unfortunately, I won't be congratulating you by name to give you the recognition you deserve for doing such a great job after our training. You'll still know it's you, though!

Congratulations!

CONTENTS

A Note From The General Manager

Joe Verde started Joe Verde Sales & Management Training, Inc., in 1985, and he became the number one automotive sales trainer in the car business with his first training class in Anaheim, California.

The reasons are simple...

Joe's methods are clear, concise, timeless and proven.
And most important to you – they're repeatable – time after time,
with today's prospects, no matter which product you sell.

Even after working with Joe for 25 years, I'm always amazed at the incredible opportunities the car business offers anyone who is serious enough to dig in, learn Joe's methods and philosophy, and has the self-discipline to master his techniques and use them on a daily basis.

Joe has developed, written, and held sales and management training in the automobile business throughout North America. We've held thousands of our own workshops, plus hundreds of special events for state, local and other associations and for dealer groups and automobile manufacturers around the world.

More people have used Joe's training
than any other automotive trainer.

Joe Verde Pioneered Online Training!

Joe was the first automotive trainer to bring Web-based training to the forefront as a new training tool for every salesperson, manager, dealer or manufacturer who wants to improve unit sales, gross and net profit, and CSI.

His online training network, JVTN.com, has all of the training and tools anyone needs to become a professional in sales or management. Over 5,500,000 (5.5 million) chapters of his training have been taken by managers and salespeople to improve their skills and their production. This year alone, more than 1.5 million chapters will be taken online by salespeople and managers who want to grow.

The Undisputed Leader In Training!

Our company, Joe Verde Sales & Management Training, Inc., is the most recognized, most recommended automotive sales, management and leadership training company in the world.

Recovery & Growth...

Joe Verde also led the charge in the car business to help as many dealers as possible recover, stabilize and grow during, and after the recession. His book, "A Dealer's Guide To Recovery & Growth," is currently in its 4th printing, and has helped thousands of dealers survive and thrive during the worst recession in our industry.

If you want to improve and grow, Joe Verde is a Master Businessman, Salesperson, Manager, Trainer and Coach and he will teach you everything you need to know to succeed in sales and sales management in the automobile industry today.

Kathleen Rittmaster

General Manager

Who Is This Book For?

This book is for everyone looking for that perfect sales job, and selling cars is it. Why? Because becoming an automotive sales professional...

- offers a flexible schedule
- is virtually 'recession proof' if you build your customer base
- doesn't require any investment for tools
- offers an unlimited income that *you* control
- lets you spend your days talking to people about cars
- means you sell a product everybody owns that people want to replace every 4 years
- and most important, it's the one job and the one profession that you can take with you anywhere you choose to live

Selling cars offers all of the benefits above and many more that I'll explain as we go. Wow, that sounds good, but there has to be a catch. Sure, there's a catch. There are three big ones selling cars...

- Commission only (until you learn to become consistent)
- The hours (until you develop your skills and get good)
- The education (you'll need this in any profession)

I'll show you how to easily handle commission only, and show you why you'll never want a 'guaranteed' salary or hourly wage again.

On your hours; *you* control those. Sure there's a schedule, but how long you work is determined by your skill level and work habits. If you don't know much, and if you don't really work, there's no rocket science here; you'll have to work longer to make a buck.

Your education requirements depend on your goals. Low goals; no need. Big goals; learn more. It's incredibly easy to learn how to earn a hundred thousand per year in sales, compared to any other profession.

While you don't need to spend a hundred grand to get a degree, it's *critical* you get the *proper initial training*, or you'll likely end up below average and statistically earn about the same as a high school dropout. After you develop your core skills, there's still more to learn, and that's best done at home or in the dealership.

Who can become a high achiever in sales?

Teachers – Factory Workers – Bankers – Farmers – Coal Miners
Military Personnel – Technicians – Nurses – Bartenders – Students

A–N–Y–B–O–D–Y

Can Learn To Become A Professional In Sales.

What's the income potential selling cars?

Unlimited is such a vague word. Here are some general guidelines...

1. Average: $20,000 to $50,000...Show up, don't really learn much about how to sell, put in long hours but spend most of your day waiting for someone to talk to, and take shortcuts whenever you can.

2. Semi-Pros: $50,000 to $100,000...You can get lucky and make $10,000 in a month – but you don't get lucky and have a $100,000 year. That takes determination, discipline and skills.

   a. On the low end, learn just a little more than what the salespeople in group #1 (above) know, go to work to work, put in some heavy hours, assume everyone's a buyer, and just treat all of your customers like you'd want to be treated if you were spending $30,000 on a purchase.

   b. On the high end, dig in and learn more than 2a. Really go to work to work, track what you do so you know what to improve, set clear goals with detailed plans, work your plan, and learn to prospect for new business and follow-up everyone who doesn't buy to get them back in.

3. The Pros In Sales: $100,000+...I've talked to people who are currently earning over $450,000 even in this market, but I'm sure there are salespeople who earn even more than that in this group of high achievers.

   The sales pros know the secret to joining this club is having the goals, determination, education, skills, discipline and integrity to reach these levels.

So what is your goal?

What are you trying to accomplish in your sales career?

- Are you changing careers and thinking about selling cars?

  If so, this book covers exactly what you need to understand and learn about this job to succeed. I'll cover the potential you have in earnings, the traps you'll have to avoid, and the skills you'll need to become a professional in sales.

- Are you selling cars now – but not earning enough? Do you want to sell more and earn more money?

  Then this book is for you. I'll walk you through this profession, and help you identify where you're hung up and why, and exactly what you need to do to get on track, or back on track fast.

- Are you selling cars now, doing really well – and want to improve even more?

  Then you'll love the book, too, because I'll remind you of all those things you can still do that you haven't done yet so you can sell even more cars, have even more fun, and make even more money – year after year.

Regardless of your motives,
one thing I can promise you is that...

Selling cars will be the highest paying,
easiest work you'll ever do...or selling cars will be
one of the lowest paying, hardest jobs you'll ever have!

I'll show you how to turn a potentially tough job selling cars into the fun, rewarding and profitable profession it can be.

My Goal With This Book

My overall goal with this book is to help you become a professional in sales. To do that, my other goals are simple. In this book, I will...

- Explain the *potential and opportunities* selling cars offers you, so that you can plan a successful and rewarding career.

- Give you an overview of *the core skills you'll need to succeed* and the information on how to develop those skills quickly.

- Cover the *problems that hold most salespeople back,* so that you can avoid the pitfalls and enjoy the rewards of your hard work.

- Clearly explain the *three success skills* you have to master if you're serious about earning a six-figure income in sales.

- Help you define your *goals* and develop the *knowledge, skills, discipline, determination and integrity* that it takes to become a professional in sales in the automobile industry.

Why should you listen to me?

Because 'I've been there – done that' on everything you'll face in this business. I've been the average salesperson who struggled and the superstar who had fun. I know exactly what *you* have to do if you want to become a professional in sales, and are serious about earning those $100,000+ paychecks every year.

Before I started selling cars, I was a very positive and disciplined person. Once I started selling cars, I fell into the traps we'll talk about in here and quickly became not only an average producer; I wasted five years because I didn't know what to do.

For my first five years, selling cars was one of the biggest struggles in my life and the most frustrating five years I've ever spent doing anything. I was that 8-car guy I refer to in our training, and I only earned $23,000 my best year. We had no training in my first dealership, no support and I learned just about everything you could possibly learn about how *not* to succeed in sales.

I worked hard, but that wasn't enough. I didn't get the education I needed to succeed. And if you don't get yours, it's almost guaranteed you'll get stuck in that 8-car guy skill-set and 8-car guy mind-set in sales, just like me, and 80% of the other salespeople in this business.

I quit selling cars after my first five years and then I spent two years learning how to sell professionally.

When I started selling cars again, I sold more units and earned more $$$ in just my first 7 months back in sales, than in my first five years combined!

I'm going to explain what I learned that took me from being that "average Joe" in sales to a high achiever overnight. (Pun intended.) And whether you're new, struggling, or already a high achiever – I'll lay out everything you need to do to reach your next level in sales.

There is so much to learn about the selling profession today, and so much to learn tomorrow to stay on top of your game, it's tough to squeeze it all into such a short book – and I can't.

To cover as much as I can, I've included tips from my books "How To Sell A Car Today", "A Dealer's Guide To Recovery & Growth," and key topics from our 2-Day Sales, 2-Day Closing & Negotiation, and 2-Day Business Development Courses, plus information from hundreds of hours of our training on JVTN®.

This book is not the end of your education, only the beginning. Next you'll need to develop your basic core skills. Then it will be your continuing education on closing, negotiation, phone and Internet, retention and your follow-up and prospecting skills that control your unit sales and income, year after year.

I've learned the real keys to success in sales are...
Clear Goals – Education – Skills – Discipline – Integrity

If you'll attend our workshops and train on JVTN® daily, and then work harder than anybody else will for the next 5 years, you'll earn more than almost anybody else can, the rest of your life.

CHAPTER 1

Why Are You In Sales?

I ask because almost everyone I've met started selling cars the same way; accidentally.

Selling cars was not my lifelong dream. In fact, I never even thought about selling cars, until the day I started. I just needed a job and found an ad in the newspaper.

Whether you're considering the car business as a new profession, or have been selling cars for years and are just ready to improve and grow to your next level, let's see what you can learn from my experiences and my mistakes the first five years I sold cars.

Take good notes throughout this book, and I'll show you how to earn over $100,000 – every year.

Everybody Has A Story

I'm originally from a small town in Texas. If you know where Brownwood, Texas is – I didn't live there. I grew up in a town *close* to Brownwood; Early, Texas. Population then: 916. And I didn't actually live in Early either, I lived on a farm 8 miles out of town.

While farm life was sort of fun, it was pretty boring most of the time. But I also developed lifelong skills that make or break success, and it was a great way to develop a strong work ethic. By the time I was in high school, about all I could think about was how I could escape the farm. And the only way to escape back then, especially with no skills of any kind except farming, was to join the military.

So I joined the Army in search of adventure!

Unfortunately, instead of adventure, 6 months later I ended up in the middle of the desert 30 miles outside of El Paso, as the company clerk, because I had learned how to type in high school.

I was creative though, so I volunteered for a job I knew would get me out of working in an office. I knew that becoming a Helicopter Mechanic would mean an immediate reassignment. Unfortunately, the only location for reassignment back then was in Vietnam, but that still sounded better than being in an office all day.

I spent my next few months in Virginia learning how to work on helicopters and then I spent my next 809 days (2 years, 2 months and 19 days) in Vietnam.

Straight from the pan into the fire...

Wow! I knew working on helicopters would be different than typing, but talk about jumping out of the frying pan and into the fire; I forgot somebody would be shooting at us most of the day. So the fun of flying around in helicopters wore off after a couple of years.

When I got back from Vietnam, I was stationed in California and after 7 years in the Army, like farming, that fun had worn off, too. So in 1972, I decided it was time to get out of the Army.

Oops – I have a family to feed and no job!

At twenty-six years old, with no money and a family to feed, I took a quick job as a bartender until I could find something.

That job paid pretty well (in nickels, dimes and quarters) and I did it for one year, exactly. Why did I quit after a year? I got tired of listening to the same drunks, who sat on the same bar stools, telling the same stories every night.

Now I have three skills I can't use...

Farming, fixing helicopters and bartending had all been good to me, but I didn't want to do any of those jobs again. I wanted to make good money though, and knew I'd have to get some kind of training, so I started looking at the jobs in the paper that offered both *good money* and *training.*

I soon realized that in the newspaper, the highest paying jobs were almost all in the 'Selling Section'. Oh sure, there were quite a few jobs that paid well in other sections, but they didn't offer any training. I don't ever recall seeing an ad for a Bank President, that said, "No experience necessary, we train," or for a Doctor or Accountant that said, "Join our staff and earn while you learn."

But if you thumbed through the want ads, it was like hitting pay dirt in the 'Selling Section'. Almost every ad in there talked about how much BIG MONEY you could make in sales.

Then I found a perfect ad,

"No experience necessary – we train!"

This ad was from an insurance company and it read something close to, "No experience necessary, we train, earn the highest commissions in town, build a future, grow with our team." So I raced down to apply for the job and spent the entire morning in interviews and taking tests.

After talking to 3 or 4 people and after taking a couple of tests, I didn't get the job that day. It wasn't that I might not get the job; they just said they were interviewing lots of people and that I needed to come back the next day for more interviews.

Luckily, I'd circled another ad and this one was from a car dealer, and it read almost the same...

> *"No experience necessary, we train, highest commissions in town, build a future, flexible hours, demo."*

I called to make sure the job was still open and the manager said, "Yeah, but you better hurry, we only have one opening and a lot of people are applying." Before we hung up, I asked him what the 'demo' was in the ad and he told me, "It's a free car to drive." He hit my hot button. I took one look at my $200, old unfaithful, worn out, ugly red VW and said, *"Hang on to that job, I'll be right down."*

When I walked in, four of us were applying for that one job and I got pretty nervous. The insurance company wasn't even offering a free car and their hiring process took 3 to 6 weeks. So logically I figured it would take at least that long to be hired at the dealership, but I wanted the job *because I really needed that free car (demo)*.

It was a typical dealership back then. There were lots of price banners on the cars and showroom windows, there were half-dead balloons from the weekend still on some of the cars, and the salespeople were just wandering around with blank stares, while they waited for a customer.

To cut this story short...

> *It took me longer to find a parking spot than it did to be hired and trained at my first dealership.*

My interview process...

If I remember my *complete* interview at that first dealership exactly, I think the manager only asked me three questions...

> Have you ever sold cars?
>
> *No sir!*
>
> Why do you think you can?
>
> *Well, I'm a good old boy, I always liked cars, plus a neighbor one time said he thought I'd be good in sales.*
>
> When can you start?
>
> *I can start today – what kind of car do I get?*

Not only was it a real short interview, what really surprised me most was he hired 3 of the 4 of us for that one job he had open.

After we were hired, there wasn't a 2-week initial sales training program, no tour of the dealership and nobody even took us around to introduce us to the other salespeople.

My initial training...

*Our initial training lasted
almost as long as the three question interview!*

After he hired the three of us, our new manager gave us our initial training program. He didn't train us, he handed us a piece of paper, the same size as this page, with 10 handwritten topics on it.

Those 10 points were his (incorrect) version of the Steps to Selling and he told us we should memorize them. That was it. Then he said, "Okay, there's the new car lot and there's the used car lot and this is the Sales Office. Do you have any questions?" And before we could answer, he turned us loose and said, "All right, you guys get out there and make me proud."

*In less than 10 minutes I'd gone from being unemployed,
to being in sales – and I'd already been trained.*

The huddle was waiting for me...

The good news, or in real life, the bad news is that when he said, *"Get out there,"* we did. We found a bunch of the other salespeople on the used car lot where they were having one of the many motivational sessions they held each day.

If you've been selling cars for more than a day or two, you know the meetings I'm referring to; those (not so) positive meetings where they talk about how great it is to be in sales, how much they love the car business, about how great the market is for their product right now, how great their managers are to work with, how fair managers always are on trade-in values and deals, and especially how fast Finance is when they finally get a deal closed. Positive, motivating meeting? Oh yeah, sure it was!

Free Membership to the Club…

All new people want to fit in – and that's one of the first errors most salespeople make, and I made it too. Because I didn't know anything about selling, or anything about the car business or what it took to succeed, it never dawned on me that I should be careful with whom I was fitting in. Why? Easy, since the dealership had no Initial Training Program or any Continuing Education, the salespeople in the huddle would become my teachers in sales.

Nice people, but definitely underachievers…

The huddle training staff was made up of nice people, but they were mostly 6-car guys. There were a couple of 8-car guys and a 10-car guy now and then, but in real life, this was just a bunch of nice people who had become underachievers in sales from their lack of education and training. They'd get together several times a day to visit and especially to justify why they weren't selling more.

Our Director of Training…

I always kid around in class about how one of the guys in the huddle volunteered for the 'Director of Training' position in the group. Who do you think that was? Who had the experience and the time and took the new guys under his wing and taught us everything he knew? If you just said the 6-car guy, you're right. Why him? Because he was the one with the most free time.

But I still had my enthusiasm…

Like everyone reading this, I started selling cars with some fear but I also had tons of enthusiasm, and that alone helped me sell.

In less than 60 days though, they stole all of my enthusiasm and taught me everything they knew about selling and success; which if you realize who was doing the training was – *zero, zip, nothing!*

**Even worse – they taught me how to rationalize
and justify why <u>not</u> selling more cars wasn't my fault.**

All it took was one BIG voucher
to get me hooked on commission sales!

Enthusiasm is your most powerful sales tool and before the huddle stole it from me, I was giving every person I talked to my very best, and most excited presentation and demonstration.

Because of my enthusiasm alone, I sold one of those converted vans with the nice shag-carpeted walls and floors, with a sunroof and an awesome 8-track stereo. And best of all, I made more money on that one sale than I made in almost two weeks in the Army. In fact, I was so excited I went straight to my new friends in the *huddle* to show them my commission voucher.

Now let's have some fun. Let's see if you can pick from the responses below how my new friends in the huddle responded to my big sale and to my new good fortune...

❑ *Wow, Joe, you did great! (Smiles and high-5s everywhere.) You keep that up, and you'll turn pro and make huge money in sales.*

❑ *So what – big deal, you just got lucky. You got a lay down, hang in there and you'll be down here with us soon.*

If you picked 'lucky' and 'laydown', you're correct. Those were the two key words in every response from the other salespeople to shoot down anything positive that happened. *Why did I listen to them?* Because like most people, I kept looking to my friends at work for support, and my friends did their best to bring me down.

My new friends threw negative bombs everywhere to start turning my head and it worked. In less than 60 days, I was voted the leader of the huddle because I was now the most negative person there.

But I was also the #1 Salesperson!

Being #1 was definitely not the big deal I thought it was back then. It's true, I was usually #1 in the store, but that just meant I was more consistent at being the 8-car guy than anybody else. I think 13 or 14 units was my personal best those first five years.

Any success I actually had back then didn't come from being good though – I could just outwork everybody else.

How important was price?

Price was no more important back then than it is now. (It means nothing if you learn to sell). But learning how to drop the price and then learning how to *hang in there and grind out a low gross deal* was almost all I was ever taught about selling my first five years...

- Our ads in the newspaper were always about how cheap we could sell a vehicle, never about the value of owning them.

- Our showroom windows had huge banners or painted signs about how cheap all of our products were. My favorite was, "Pile 'em Deep, Sell 'em Cheap!"

- We also had discounts marked on the windshield in white shoe polish to further remind our prospects that cheap was the most important message about our products and our dealership.

- In case they missed the paper, didn't see the banners and the windshield was clean, every vehicle had a red tag special hanging on the rear view mirror to remind them...*we are cheap!*

Price ads are to draw a crowd...

As bad as price advertising is, it does bring people into the dealership, so it works. But our managers never taught us how to move away from the price and back to selling value, once we had a customer. So we cheap-sold every vehicle, and tried to grind out a low gross deal in those 5-hour negotiation marathons.

Even our greeting focused on price...

> *Welcome to ABC Motors, if we could find a car you like and work it out the way you want to buy it, would you take it home today?*

If they said 'No', we asked again...

> *But if we gave you our best deal, would you buy it now?*

And if they said 'No' again, we just handed them our 'dismissal slip' (business card) and as they were leaving we said...

> *Before you buy anywhere else, make sure you*
> *see us first, because we'll beat any deal in town.*

We didn't give good presentations or even demo people unless we had to. Our only goal was to get them to agree to buy a car at any price and then get them inside, so our manager could try to close the sale for us – on price, of course.

Sure we sold some cars, or to be more accurate some people bought in spite of our skills. But we didn't make any money and you won't either, if you only focus on price and don't sell the value of ownership.

In my first tour of duty selling cars, I sold for five years, but the fun started to wear off with those 7-day work weeks and 10 to 12 hour days. I know a lot of you work bell to bell, but our bell didn't ring at night until there were no more prospects on the lot, and I was there many nights until 2 or 3 a.m., still trying to hammer out that price-focused deal, only to end up with a $12 voucher, all too often. (We had 'minis', but they were waived without notice.)

Our price-focused process turned every negotiation into a game and if you make it a game, too, I guarantee you'll find a ton of prospects who want to play, and some of them are *real good at it.*

If you'll notice, when you only sell price, it's a lot like playing the slot machines or blackjack in Vegas; you just can't win often enough or big enough to make a lot of money.

Our Closing Question:

Would you – would you – would you?

I was taught the least effective ways to close. We were taught to just keep asking, "If we could work it out the way you want to buy it, will you take it home today?" over and over again, in different ways.

Worse, I was taught through experience that selling was doing whatever it takes to *push and pressure* people until you wore them down, so they'd sign on the dotted line.

Our only goal was to get any kind of commitment to buy, no matter what it took, and then get them signed up and over the curb before they changed their minds. After delivery, we never contacted them again, because we knew most of them were not happy.

We practiced confrontational selling at its best!

The selling style I was taught was definitely *confrontational.* And since that's what I was taught from day one in my new profession, I never considered whether it made sense or not.

But if you slow down and think for just a minute – who in their right mind would ever use a confrontational style of selling and expect very many people to buy the product? Duh – when you push people, they push back, and you lose sales!

I Give Up – I'm Tired – I Quit!

I was getting tired of selling cars and just getting tired, period. But I still thought the money was pretty good. In those first five years (in the late seventies), I was averaging about $1,500 per month and my best year was $23,000. When you factor in inflation, I was making just about what an average salesperson earns today.

I justified that the money was worth putting in the long hours. Besides, I was the top salesperson almost every month and I was making a lot of money, or at least that's what I thought.

Then one day I was playing around with a calculator and decided to figure out how much I made per hour. I entered my income and divided it by the 70 or 80 hours we were working each week. When the answer came up, I figured I'd gotten a bad calculator, because it obviously couldn't do math.

So I did the math again, and again, and again – then I quit selling cars the next day. Why? Because...

I'd been confusing what I was making
with how long I was working.

I realized I was making less than minimum wage, and I was earning less money per hour than the kid working at Biggee Burger. I realized that I was only making decent money overall because I was working the equivalent of two full-time jobs. Even worse...

I found out I wasn't an 8-car guy like I thought I was.
I realized I was just a 4-car guy working double shifts!

I really wasn't interested in working two jobs to make $1,500.

The next day I quit my job in the highest paying profession, and the best industry in the country. And the worst part for me and for everyone else who has quit selling cars for those same reasons, is that because I never got the proper training and education, *I never even knew how much opportunity I really had selling cars.*

There were a lot of things I did like about selling cars, though. In fact, I liked just about everything about the car business my first five years except: *the image, the hours, the pay and the customers.*

Most people get the first three, but why didn't I like customers?

Because they weren't very friendly. After we blocked their trade-ins, turned them six times and started pushing them into buying a car they weren't sure they wanted, for more than they meant to spend, go figure – they got mad at us! Some even called the Police.

Now I have to find another new career...

Actually, I made the decision on my new profession the same day I quit selling cars. I'd gotten to know the guy who did our pinstriping and side moldings and I asked him if I could work with him. He said, "No." So I said, "What if I work for 30 to 60 days FREE while you teach me the business?" Besides, I figured it would be fun and I'd still be outside around cars.

*I think it was offering to work for **FREE** that cinched the deal.*

I worked with George, he taught me the business and soon I was out on my own. After farming, Vietnam, bartending and selling cars, I definitely knew how to put in long hours.

So being a hard worker, it didn't take long before I started to build some good accounts and sell more products. But I had a problem. I learned how to pinstripe, but didn't know how to run a business and I didn't know anything about accounting.

More important, I knew that even the wisest 6-car guy couldn't help with this one, so I went to a bookstore to find a couple of books on accounting and on how to grow my business.

**When I walked into the bookstore that day,
I was in my early 30s, and I had less than $500!**

Like hard workers everywhere with good intentions, I had put in tons of hours for five years and (I thought) I had honestly given selling cars my very best shot.

For five years every tip about selling from my managers had been: *You should, you need to, you ought to...*

Even though all of our advertising was on price, my managers had told me several things again and again those first five years. They said: *I should, I needed to, that I ought to do lots of things, like...*

- Stop talking about price and build value

- Control your prospects and give them good presentations

- Get some minor commitments from them as we went along

- Follow-up with the people who didn't buy to get them back in

- Turn those phone calls into appointments when people call in

- Go out and bring some of your own customers in

So I'd try to do those things, but here's how it would go: My manager would grind me about talking price all the time, so I'd spend more time with the next prospect like he said. Then he'd yell at me for spending too much time with them..."Hurry up and find out what they want to spend. You've been with those people for 10 minutes and we've got people all over the lot!"

Or he'd say, "Verde – find out what they want for their trade before you spend any more time with them." Plus he kept repeating, "There's no such thing as a be-back," over and over again, so why would I ever do any follow-up?

Besides yelling at me when I actually did what he told me to do, the other problem was that he never, ever, even one time, showed me *how* to do any of those things he told me I *should be* doing. And he never, ever offered me any kind of outside training or recommended a sales book or anything else so I could learn to do what he wanted.

Have you ever been in a bookstore?

I hadn't! I was 30 something and I had actually done my best to avoid bookstores. We didn't have Book Super Stores then with a Coffee Shop inside to lure us in. Plus all they had in bookstores were books, and I wasn't much into reading books.

Shock and Awe!

When I walked into that first bookstore to get my book on accounting, I was shocked to find hundreds of books on how to sell, close, overcome objections, follow-up, prospect, use the phones, control your success, set goals, and on how to run a business.

I found books in there on everything that I was supposed to be doing the last five years in sales. And the best part – they were logical and made sense. Plus, none of them were written by a 6-car guy.

The only problem was that they were all on selling stuff like Insurance, or Real Estate or some other product – not cars.

Holy Smokes – What A Difference An Education Makes!

For the next 2 years that I had my accessory business, I spent every free minute reading books, writing my notes, and converting what I was learning about selling Houses, Insurance, and Pots and Pans into *scripts* (the words) I could use selling Cars.

Some of you may have heard of that really, really old dead-guy named Socrates. He, too, was a master at communication and it took me a long time to figure out what Socrates was talking about when he said...

> **"If you want people to say the right thing,
> just ask them the right question."**

But as I read more, I finally caught on, and I learned that selling is a logical and repeatable process anyone can learn, and that it works with almost all of the people, almost all of the time. I learned that by following the same correct steps every time with every prospect, you can sell most people what they came to buy.

One of the Masters of Success was Napoleon Hill, and there's a longer story than we can cover here about how he learned and developed his skills in sales and about how he became so successful. But he told all of us how we could also become Masters in Sales...

"If you'll spend an hour each day learning about your profession, in three years, you'll be a Master in your field." – Napoleon Hill

Napoleon Hill, J. Douglas Edwards, Art Linkletter, W. Clement Stone, Ben Franklin, Plato, Socrates and a hundred other great people were my teachers and helped me learn how to succeed.

All of these men had reached the highest levels of success in sales and in business, and every one of them presented the same exact common sense approach to selling and success, even though they lived and died centuries apart.

The single most important selling concept I learned is that...

Selling is 100% enthusiasm, 93% process, and 7% product!

If you will *learn and enthusiastically follow* the selling process, you can sell any product at a professional level and earn professional wages in that field. But if you can't *sell*, no amount of smiles or product knowledge will get you to the top in this profession.

From these most successful people, I learned you don't have to drop the price to overcome objections. Even more important, I learned that when you drop the price, you lower the value of your product. That means dropping the price makes overcoming a legitimate price objection even tougher to handle.

I was also surprised to discover that my two favorite closes, "If I could work it out, would you buy it?" and "Do y'all want to go inside and see what we can do?" are the worst *type* of closing questions you could ever ask and they cost you sales every month.

If you want to do well in sales, on 'price' remember that...

You don't miss sales because of a few dollars,
you miss sales because of a few words!

I also learned that if you're selling an expensive product like cars, that people buy again and again, follow-up and prospecting are your keys to success. Unsold follow-up and prospecting will help you put more people on the lot right now to help you make more sales today. A solid sold customer follow-up and a retention process will help you build your business for tomorrow.

It's important to understand that success in sales (and in life) is a journey, not a destination. That's why having daily, monthly, yearly and lifetime goals is critical. I've seen so many people give up on sales and themselves because they started slow. I've also seen just as many start out like shooting stars, only to burn out just as fast. None of these salespeople had a longer term goal than *right now*.

Whether you're new or have been selling cars for 30 years, how many (or how few) units you sell in your first 60 or 90 days, or first 30 years has almost no impact on how successful you'll become tomorrow, if you just keep learning more today.

When you're learning how to sell and learning how to become successful, it helps to remember...

Success is a marathon, not a 100 yard dash.
Starting slow doesn't mean you'll lose the race,
and starting fast doesn't mean you'll win.

There Are Two Secrets To Success...
Developing Core Skills And Continuing Education!

Our beliefs control our success.

From the huddle and from my own experience, I had always believed that the market, the weather, the economy, the competition, our advertising – especially being able to offer the lowest price within driving distance – determined my success selling cars. Because I worked hard, if things didn't work out, it must not have been my fault.

I also believed that because I had been the #1 salesperson most months and since I only averaged about 8 units, that logically, 8 units must be good, and 8 must be about as many units as anybody could expect to sell on a regular basis.

Sure, I knew I could get lucky now and then and hit 12 or 13 one month. But realistically, I believed that anybody who could average 8 or 10 units was doing a good job.

I Was Arrogantly Average!

We were talking about how average and below average salespeople believe the same things I did, and a Dealer in our management class said some of his salespeople had become arrogantly average. He said they not only couldn't sell, but were extremely arrogant about how well they thought they were doing.

Boy, did he hit the nail on the head describing me those first five years.

I was so arrogant about my *perceived* skill level in sales that I couldn't hear somebody even if they were trying to teach me easy ways to improve. Plus, I had no role models in sales to learn from.

During my first five years, I never met anyone who sold more than 10 or 12 units consistently. Sure I'd heard of a couple of guys who sold 20 or so. But the *huddle lied to me* and told me those guys were either in fleet, got all the house deals, or that they were related to the owner – and that's the only reason they were more successful.

After I learned about selling, I realized that all of us had been lied to by the untrained huddle before us, who were lied to by the untrained huddle before them. Worse, not only did we lie to each other; we lied to ourselves and our families about why we weren't putting more bread on the table and more money in the bank.

OK, lying may be too harsh a word, since we weren't lying to each other on purpose. It was just all we knew and more important, it was what we wanted to hear, because it gave us an 'out' on why we didn't sell more. Whatever our reasons, we were definitely not telling the truth about why we weren't selling more.

I don't know about you, but I can remember telling my family that I was real sorry we couldn't get that new car, or that nicer house and I can remember carefully *justifying* why I didn't buy my son more presents at Christmas or for his birthday.

It was always...

> *"Son, I'm sorry I couldn't get that bicycle you wanted this year, but it's been tough in sales – nobody's buying, the market is bad, my managers aren't helping me, plus the competition is killing us."*

Sound familiar? I never remember telling my wife or my son the real reasons I wasn't selling more and bringing home more money...

"Son, I'm sorry I couldn't get you that bike – and honey, I'm sorry we didn't get a vacation again this year, or move to that bigger apartment, and I'm really bummed you have to drive a car with no windows on the right side, but to be honest, Daddy's kinda lazy. I could sell a lot more cars if I just went to work to work, but I screw around most of the day, visit with my friends, and just wait for somebody to show up – that's why I have to work so many hours and work my days off.

Plus when I finally get someone to talk to, I take shortcuts and pre-qualify people instead of giving all of them a good presentation and demo. And I really don't like doing follow-up or prospecting so I miss sales there, too. And I don't know why, but I also hate taking incoming sales calls, so I miss out on a lot of sales there each month. And while I'm being so honest, I don't know enough about 'selling' to close a door with a spring on it, much less a sale. But I love you guys, though."

How about you?

What did you tell your family last Christmas?

What will you tell them this Christmas?

Earn Over $100,000 Selling Cars

Let's finish the story...

When I learned to sell, manage and run a business, my accessory business was going gang busters. In less than two years, I'd built one of the two or three largest mobile accessory companies in LA and Orange County. I even opened a retail shop right across from the Irvine Auto Mall where I had most of the dealerships as customers.

I was learning all these great things about selling and how to sell pinstripes and stuff, but it wasn't the same great feeling you get selling cars, and I really missed that *rush*.

There's nothing more fun than meeting a stranger who doesn't like you, know you or trust you (yet), and then moving through their initial objections, making friends, gradually getting control of the sale, gathering the information you need to present, demonstrate, close the sale, and overcome their objections – and then watching them drive away in a brand new vehicle a few hours later, smiling and thanking you for helping. That, and the money, of course.

What really motivated me to get back into selling cars was that I'd be on the lot doing $10 pinstripes and listening to salespeople miss selling opportunities left and right, and blowing $500 commissions because they'd had no training on how to listen, or how to sell.

Now it's time to go back to the future...

When I first started selling cars again, I was still working full days in my accessory business and I could only sell cars a few hours each day. But selling cars part-time my first month, I sold 18 units and about the same number my second month, which was also my *last* month of doing both jobs.

I realized I couldn't commit to two jobs and do either of them at the level I expected of myself. So a couple of months later I got rid of my accessory business and I started selling cars again full time. *In my first 7 months back in the car business full time* – with my new improved selling skills and my renewed enthusiasm...

> **I sold more units and made more money in 7 months**
> **than I did my entire first 5 years combined!**

Whether you're brand new, stuck at 8 units, or consistently averaging 20 or 30 plus right now, I understand exactly where you're at, because I've been there, too.

So if you're just starting and want that 'fast start', or if you're trying to climb your way out of some rut to get your career on track, or if you want to move to your next level as an even higher achiever, I know exactly how to help you do that, too, and that's exactly what this book is about.

I know the challenges you're going to face developing your skills, getting organized, and building your business, and I know exactly how to walk you through the process, step-by-step. But there's a catch; you'll have to do something that keeps most salespeople from growing – you'll have to quiet down those little negative voices in your head that will keep popping up reminding you of those 'yeah, buts' we've all bought into, and just follow my directions, instead.

If you'll learn from my mistakes and my success over the last 30 years, I'll show you how to sell more cars, have more fun, and I'll show you how to make more money than you've ever imagined!

Before You Read Any Further

1. Get a 3-ring binder, a highlighter and pen or pencil.

2. Go back through all of the previous pages and highlight everything you realize that I did wrong, or wasn't taught my first five years that kept me from selling more, that you're also doing now. (Do the same thing after every chapter.)

3. Start a section in your notebook called: "Improvements I Need To Make" and add everything you just highlighted to your list.

4. Add a second section titled: "Improvements I've Made" and as you work on and improve your skills, add to that section, too.

Then as we go through the rest of the book, I'll show you where and how to make those changes. Now slow down and read the next page carefully, because your next choices completely control your success.

Your Success Is All About Your Choices!

One of the books I read early on was a book called "Choices" by Shad Helmstetter. I didn't like it, because it reminds all of us about the choices we're faced with in life.

Example: When you honestly don't realize you could sell more by doing follow-up, technically you're off the hook about why you aren't selling more cars.

But once you understand that more follow-up logically equals more sales and a higher income, then if you choose not to follow-up – you've chosen not to sell more units and chosen not to earn more. *Becoming aware makes it a choice.*

From reading "Choices" I realized that literally *everything* in life and about selling is a choice. You choose to go to work and do your best every day or you choose to hang around all day and wait for something to happen.

You choose to give that next prospect your best presentation, or you choose not to. And if you choose not to work, and not to give great presentations to every prospect, then by default, *you choose not to increase your sales or your income.*

You'll also choose to attend our classes for your initial training and choose to train daily on JVTN®, or you'll choose not to. That single choice will determine your level of success, and I'll explain why in the very next chapter.

'Sales' is full of potential and you can accomplish any goal you set and you can earn any amount of money you want to earn. It's really pretty simple, just choose to learn more every day, choose to give it your very best every day at work, and you'll earn more every year.

"It's only when you exercise your right to <u>choose</u>, that you can also exercise your right to <u>change</u>!"
– Choices

CHAPTER 2

Your Potential Selling Cars

Potential:

Noun: The capacity or ability for future achievement!

Let's talk about the real potential you have to sell a lot of cars and to make a lot of money in today's market.

Why focus on potential? Because one of the most important things in hitting the big time in sales is believing you can. And then, as you start to improve in sales, you have to learn how to think even BIGGER as you grow, so you can keep seeing how you can continue to improve for the rest of your career.

Who Sells Cars?

First, let's look at two areas: who sells cars, and how much money they make. Then, we'll talk about the real potential you have in sales in your market, if you're serious about hitting the big time.

Over 3,000 Salespeople Surveyed Online

We started a general survey in 2002, and immediately saw that the income from salespeople who'd taken our training was way higher than for the salespeople who hadn't. In 2006, we added questions about our online training, JVTN®. The difference between salespeople who have never used Joe Verde training and the salespeople who attend our classes and use JVTN® is astounding.

We also learned more about those 3,355 salespeople than just about their units and income. Let's look at a few other facts we learned from our online survey about salespeople in the car business...

Online Survey Of 3,355 Salespeople – General Statistics

- Average age is 34.69 years

- 91% are male, 9% are female

- 38% came from a 'commission sales' background

- 59% chose the car business because of the income potential

- 29.8% were referred into the business…32% answered an ad

- *Reputation* was why 23.2% picked their current dealership

- 57% sell domestic, 32% imports and 11% sell high line imports

- 5.5 More Units: The average salesperson said they could sell 5.5 more units per month if they just applied themselves at work each day, even without more training.

- 7.3 Hours of Training: The average salesperson only received 7.3 hours of training when they were hired into one of the highest paying professions in the country, and they rated their Initial Training a 4.4 on a scale of 1 to 10.

How Well Do They Do?

**Online Survey
Performance Statistics**

Survey Results 2002 - 2005

A. <u>No Joe Verde Training</u>

Salespeople who <u>did not</u> use any of our training or attend any of our workshops:

Sold ....9.7 units per month

Earned ....$3,710 per mo / $44,520 per year

B. <u>With Joe Verde Training</u>

Salespeople who attended our workshops from 2002 – 2005: (JVTN® was not yet available.)

Sold ....12.3 units per month

Earned ....$5,821 per mo / $69,852 per year

Survey Results 2006 - Present

A. <u>No Joe Verde Training</u>

Sell ....9.7 units per month

Earn ....$3,774 per mo / $45,288 per year

B. <u>With Joe Verde Training: Workshops and/or JVTN®</u>

Sell ....12.0 units per month

Earn ....$8,746 per mo / $104,952 per year

The facts mean that you can average a 22% increase in your unit sales and earn at least $104,952 per year with our training. The best part – if you're really motivated, you'll do even better!

Why did incomes double, even though # of units are only up 22%?

That is the first question these numbers usually prompt with most salespeople, and there's a logical answer...

- Learning to sell means learning to build value in your product. When you learn how to follow The New Basics™, you learn how to warm up the prospect and give better presentations and demonstrations, and *that means more value.*

- Building more value throughout the sale logically *increases the gross profit.*

- Learning to close the sale on the value of owning the product, and learning to handle objections without dropping the price, also logically *increases the gross profit even more.*

- Learning how to bypass price on the lot, rephrase price when you're closing, and learning how to refocus your negotiation on budget instead of price *increases the gross profit even more.*

- Learning to develop your own customer base instead of spending a career waiting around to talk to hard to close, low gross floor traffic generated by price-focused advertising, *equals easier to close, higher gross profit deals, too. (Gross is 40% higher on repeats, referrals, and outside prospects you generate.)*

- *More bonuses!* Another couple of units per month puts you into more bonus categories more often at your dealership.

They earn more than twice as much money on just a few more units because they learned how to sell, build value, close, negotiate, and generate more of their own higher-gross floor traffic.

"I doubled my sales and gross after class."

"I more than doubled my unit sales (from 8 to 17) and my gross per unit after your class! Having those extra closes from class worked. Thanks, Joe." Dave, Salesperson, Ford, New Jersey

---

**Results from salespeople like yourself after
going through our training and using JVTN®**

We've been holding training longer, and with dramatically higher results than anyone else in this industry. It's a proven fact that when you attend our classes and train on JVTN®, you will sell more units and earn more money than the people who don't – period.

Over the years, from our training in classes, on video and now with our Online Training (JVTN®), we've had thousands of salespeople grow and improve once they learn how to sell on a professional level and follow the common sense processes we teach.

Your potential is not only unlimited, the real potential is so high, most salespeople don't believe it can possibly be true.

I've talked to, met and received hundreds of letters from salespeople after our training. Hopefully some of their dramatic improvements will help you realize you can also sell more than you are now…

- After your Sales Class, I went from 11 to 20 units and my income jumped to $15,500 last month.
- I was brand new but after watching your Fast Start Series on JVTN®, I'm already averaging 14.5 units in my 4th month.
- I never sold before attending your Sales Class in Dallas. My first day was Saturday and I delivered the only two vehicles sold that day and then I sold two more the following week.
- After going through your Fast Start Series For Salespeople on JVTN®, I doubled my sales from 8 to 16 the next month.
- After your class, I went from an 8-car guy to a 12-car guy and made an extra $14,242 over the same period last year.
- Our Finance gross is up $530 per unit from watching JVTN®. Your training has helped us build rapport and establish trust with our prospects.
- I've increased my take home pay from $3,300 to $10,900 per month just by using the techniques I learned on JVTN®.
- After your Sales Class, I sold 5 units in the next week.
- After your Sales Course, I went from 10 to 21 units.

- After using JVTN® our gross per unit is up from $2,400 to $3,900. Now salespeople stay off price, build value and get real commitments, which makes the negotiation more efficient.

- Before JVTN®, I was averaging 14 units, now I'm at 23 and my income went from $113,000 last year to $166,000 this year.

- With JVTN®, I've doubled my income by going to work to work, following Joe's Basics and maintaining a great attitude.

- Last year at the RV show, I only sold 3 coaches. This year after being on JVTN® I sold 7. This training really works!

- With your training, in the last 60 days, I'm up to 15 units per month, my commission is up from $416 per unit to $766 and at that, I'm on track to earn $150,000 in the next 12 months.

- Five of our salespeople *doubled* their sales and increased their gross 40% in just 30 days thanks to your training on JVTN®.

- After your sales course, my salesperson went from 7 to 21.5. Not bad for a guy who worked at a fast food place a few months ago.

- After training, we cut advertising 25%, increased units 25% and gross and CSI are higher than ever.

- We've sent salespeople to other training, and they had fun. We went to your course and developed skills. Now like you say; my guys have even more fun, sell more cars, and make more money.

- Our newest salesperson started with your Fast Start Series on JVTN®, and within 6 months has a 22 unit average.

- I sold 40% more boats at the show this year than I sold the year before. Going to class right before the show was great.

- Our Auto and RV salespeople have had their best months ever since we started on JVTN® and one increased his gross 200%.

- My gross profit is up 25% just from watching JVTN® and learning to stay off price and tracking everything I'm doing.

- In just three months, my salesperson went from 8 to 20 units after your class and he did it without taking any floor traffic.

- In the last three months, I've averaged 76 units per month!

And other high achievers who've been through our training...

- A salesperson delivered 116 'retail' units and earned over $80,000 that month and averaged over 80 units per month.

- A salesperson was back in class who just came off a 96 car month, who averaged about 55 units per month.

- A top Ford salesperson in the country who is averaging 40+ units per month. This next salesperson emailed us that...

- He started our training when he was earning $100,000+. The next year he hit the low $200,000s, then the high $200,000s, the next year over $300,000 and his fourth year training, he and his manager called to tell us he earned $455,000.

- A saleswoman who averages 42 units per month, works 8-5, Monday through Fridays only. (We'll talk more about her.)

- He sold 6 cars a week while he was still in the Military.

- The top Hyundai salesperson had 65.5 units on the board the first month I met him. And another salesperson...

- Earned over $400,000 last year selling only used vehicles, in a town of 15,000 people *without taking any walk-in traffic.*

- A salesperson who was #1 in his dealership for 62 months and delivered 188 units his best month.

- A GM who started as a Porter, sold 37.5 units his first month, averaged 80 per month and had many months over 100.

- A saleswoman who was averaging 8 units per month and delivered 13 the very next week after she went to our class.

- A top Lincoln Mercury salesperson who sells 40+ units.

- And a salesperson who just sent me an email said, "I earned $1,444,000 selling cars in 4-1/2 years using the Verde System." (That's $320,888 per year.)

Again, these comments are from people who are both brand new to selling, or who had been selling for years and decided to make the change and become High Achievers in sales.

That means if they can do it, so can you – if you want it bad enough!

We get these kinds of results from the salespeople, managers and dealers we train, because they let us help them develop the *core skills* it takes to succeed – then they keep learning more on JVTN®.

Not counting our workshops each month or the 50,000 salespeople who read our newsletters each month – people have logged on and taken 5,500,000 (5.5 million) chapters on JVTN® to learn how to sell more cars, have more fun and make more money.

Are these people and their results exceptional?

Absolutely. They wanted more success, and were willing to take the time and put in the effort to attend class and then to apply what they learned.

I'd agree that most people will never hit $455,000 per year selling cars. But somebody's doing it, so if anybody tells you it isn't possible, it would be easy to believe, but it just won't be true.

Just because I can't bench press 1,000 pounds or shoot 60 in a round of golf, or run a mile in 4 minutes, doesn't make any of those achievements impossible, even if there's no way I can ever come close to *seeing* myself doing those things.

Could I increase my weights or improve my golf game *some,* though? Sure, I can find out exactly where I am now and I can definitely improve on everything *some* if I put in the effort.

In sales there are literally dozens of areas you can continually work on to get a little better now and continue to improve every month.

And with the right education, direction, self-discipline and practice, you can reach any goal you set.

> **Potential is just believing we can get even a little better
> at anything we do – so we make the effort to continually grow.**

The best part of selling cars:
Potential, with no overhead!

The really neat thing about the potential in this business is your dealer supplies almost everything you need to reach any goal you can possibly set.

Your dealership supplies you with the vehicles, a desk, a phone, the paperwork, a service department, a finance manager, a business office to take care of the paperwork and even someone to keep the cars clean and ready to sell. And your dealer didn't even ask you to take out a loan to help with the inventory.

In fact, your dealer also supplies you with enough walk-in traffic to earn $20,000 to $50,000 a year without generating any business on your own. You get all these benefits with no up-front expenses, very few skills and pretty ineffective work habits.

I think everyone would agree $20,000 to $50,000 is a pretty good base in any job. But with our training, you'll give yourself the chance to learn more so you can *earn more in a year, than many average people earn in 5 years.* Then you can continually take your skills, your work habits, your attitude and your follow-up to the next level.

By the way, if you're new and you just came from a lower paying job, I know $30,000 – $40,000 – $50,000 per year sounds like great money...but think of it as 'starting pay' in the car business. Then just keep learning more, growing and never look back.

How much more do you have to learn and how many changes do you have to make? That's completely up to you, and it all depends on your goals, and how far you want to go in sales.

Opportunity And Potential
Are Everywhere In Sales

You've stumbled upon an incredible opportunity in sales whether you sell cars, boats, motorcycles, RVs, homes, insurance or other products, because it's all about learning how to sell professionally.

Potential is everywhere and even though that's true, not everyone *chooses* to go for it. If you'll start listening more carefully though, most of the people who don't choose to grow and improve are clinging to reasons to justify why it isn't their fault and why learning more or working smarter just won't work for them.

Even when California had the big Gold Rush back in the 1800s, not everybody grabbed a shovel and headed West. I'm sure a lot of people back then, just like most salespeople in every dealership said, "It's too much trouble," "I'm too busy," "I don't have time," "I don't have the money," or any mix of a few dozen easy excuses to justify not 'going for the gold'.

In fact, one of the gold miners who did head West and struck it rich, sent his friend a letter that read...

"There's gold everywhere,
buy a pick and shovel and get here quick!"

His friend replied...

"Can't afford to – with the gold rush on, they want
way too much money for picks and shovels these days!"

The gold is there in sales, especially automobile sales. As long as you're willing to get out your pick and shovel and dig, you can start cashing in on the gold, no matter what brand you sell or what market you're in.

People will buy cars today, all of their friends will buy cars today, and all of them will buy even more cars tomorrow. They'll buy a lot of those vehicles from *you,* if you make the commitment to get your education and learn how to sell, close the sale and learn how to build your business.

"Your business is never really good or bad out there.
Your business is either good or bad right between
your own two ears." – Zig Ziglar

CHAPTER 3

Understanding Your Market
To Sell More Cars

The first step to earning over $100,000 every year is to make several assumptions about every single person who walks on the lot:

- They can buy

- They came to buy

- You will sell them a vehicle, if you do a good job

After they miss a few sales in a row, most salespeople start questioning everything about their next prospect's ability to buy just based on how they look, act or dress. They start questioning the prospect's motives for being on the lot, then start skipping the critical steps of selling because they don't *believe* the prospect can or will buy.

When the prospect leaves without buying – their belief is confirmed: "See, I knew he wasn't a buyer."

*Most Salespeople and Managers
Believe They Are In A Unique Situation!*

Human nature, input, conditioning, ego, pride – all of the above – help every one of us rationalize that while we could grow at least some, not growing usually isn't our fault. We begin to believe that our lack of success or growth really isn't as much about us as it is about the unique problems in our community or our dealership.

People who take the time to come to our classes are logically interested in growth. But at 8 a.m. the first day before our class starts, there are always a few people in the room who are skeptical. They don't think they can sell more, and they can't imagine how any training can help them overcome the unique problems in their market or with the dealership problems they have to face every day.

Some of those unique problems and situations we hear at the beginning of our classes may sound familiar to you...

- We're in the wrong part of town and don't get enough traffic
- Every incoming call / Internet lead I get is about price
- We have models in our product line that just aren't selling
- Our advertising isn't effective – we don't get enough traffic
- We advertise every vehicle and there's no gross profit left
- It isn't about value, our prospects only care about price
- People ask for the vehicles and colors we don't have in stock
- The competition is offering every vehicle under invoice
- Our market is off right now and there's nothing I can do
- We're in a small town and everybody who comes on the lot asks for _____ because he's been here so long
- We're in a small town and don't have a big draw for prospects
- We're in a large metro market – there's too much competition
- Our economy has been hard hit and people just aren't buying
- I sell the wrong products – people just aren't buying our brand

But by 10 a.m. in class, things have changed...

By the very first break, every salesperson and manager in the room has begun to realize that everyone else in the room faces almost all of the same unique problems that each of them thought only they had in their market, in their dealership.

By that same first break, from what we've already covered in just a couple of hours, everybody in the room is realizing every one of those unique situations is just a problem that can be solved.

In just a couple of hours in our sales class, every salesperson in the room is also getting a sense of the true untapped potential they really have to sell a car (or two) every single day in their market, with their product, in their dealership.

One of the biggest challenges in becoming, and consistently being a High Achiever in sales is to maintain that constant belief *every day* in the potential this business offers anyone serious about closing more sales, delivering more vehicles and building their business.

To help you with the first step – take a minute on the next few pages to do an honest evaluation about the people in your market and the potential you'll discover that you really have to sell more.

This isn't my version of your market, I'll just supply the questions. This will be *your own personal evaluation* of what you think about your market and your potential for selling cars.

This is one of the most important chapters in the book, so take the time to really think about each question.

***Understanding your potential is critical to your growth.
So go slow, there's no rush!***

> *"After attending Joe's 2 Day Sales Workshop and training with JVTN®, I sold 6 units my first week after class! I just started asking the right questions. I never knew selling could be this easy. Thanks." Nathan, Salesperson, Honda, Canada*

A Few Quick Questions
About Selling Cars In Your Market

Are there buyers in my community right now?

1. Except for the people who are too young or too old to drive anymore, 95% of the people in our community either own a vehicle now or will get one soon. ❑ True ❑ False

2. If #1 is true, since practically everyone in our community owns a vehicle now or will get one soon, *that makes almost everyone in our community a buyer.* ❑ True ❑ False

3. If #2 is true, since almost everyone in our community is a buyer, the only two questions there really are when someone walks on the lot, with anyone I meet on the street, with every existing customer in our database and with everyone in our service drive is...

    1) *when* they'll buy their next vehicle and...

    2) *which salesperson* will make the sale?

    ❑ True ❑ False

What about the competition I face in my market?

4. Logically, if I just do a better job of selling, building value and closing the sale than the salesperson my prospect may meet down the street, I'll sell some of the people he or she would have sold. ❑ True ❑ False

5. If #4 is true, if I just do a better job of presenting, demonstrating and closing sales than every other salesperson in town, and if I continue to learn more, I can improve my sales right now and continue to improve them every year. ❑ True ❑ False

About those price questions and objections my prospects have...

6. Whether it's just a question, a budget concern, or an objection, most of my prospects bring up price in some form, out on the lot, before they actually find a vehicle they're willing to take home today. ❑ True ❑ False

7.   It is true that price is important to almost all of us, but in the end, people make their *decision to purchase* based on the *value* they feel they'll receive for the price they have to pay, and that's based on how I do in #5 above.   ❏ True ❏ False

8.   If #7 is true and buying is based on *value* for almost every person, after my presentation and during my attempts to close the sale, if I have a prospect who honestly objects to the price – the real objection is that I didn't create enough value *to justify the price* I'm asking them to pay.   ❏ True ❏ False

About my work habits and skills in sales...

9.   Even if I get better at closing and handling objections from Joe Verde courses and JVTN®, it will still be tough to close more sales and sell a car today or to earn professional wages if I still pre-qualify people, talk price, try to take shortcuts and skip the basic steps of selling.   ❏ True ❏ False

10.   If I do my best, but still don't close the sale and a prospect leaves our dealership without buying – *if I follow-up effectively,* there's a *pretty good chance* they'll come back in and buy the vehicle from me.   ❏ True ❏ False

11.   If I didn't close the sale today, and if I *choose* not to follow-up, unfortunately statistics prove, and logic in #3 says, the prospect will end up buying their vehicle from a salesperson down the street.   ❏ True ❏ False

12.   If I *don't* follow-up every working prospect, when my prospects do buy their vehicle down the street, those other salespeople I'm sending those deals to every month will not spiff me for the referrals.   ❏ True ❏ False

13.   Even if I *never* become a lean, mean closing machine, if I just follow-up all of my working prospects and sold customers, I'll sell more vehicles each year.   ❏ True ❏ False

About experience and training...

14.   If all it took was experience (and no training) to get better at selling and closing, then someone who started selling 10 cars a month 10 years ago, should now, 10 years later, be selling 30 each month – but they usually aren't.   ❑ True   ❑ False

15.   A well-trained salesperson will almost always sell more and earn more money than a salesperson with no real training, so if I continually learn more about selling and apply what I learn, I'll continue to sell more and earn more.   ❑ True   ❑ False

16.   Most salespeople only bother to learn just enough to be average, but they do learn how to blame being average on just about everyone and everything else.   ❑ True   ❑ False

What do I think is the potential in my market, at my dealership?

17.   Based on my answers to these questions – whether I earn just average wages or whether I sell more and earn professional wages; it really isn't up to the market, the weather or my dealership. Whether I sell more and earn more depends on my selling skills, my work habits, my attitude and whether I do my follow-up and prospect with the buyers in my community to build my own business.   ❑ True   ❑ False

18.   Using what I already know, if I really applied myself each day and just did my very best job with everyone I talk to, in real life, **I could be delivering an extra _____ units per month right now.**

If you're serious about improving...

Using your number in #18 – do the math to find your real potential. Multiply the units per month times your average commission to find your monthly potential. Multiply that by 12 to see annual potential. Then multiply annual by how many more years you think you'll be working.

That final number is your potential in your market today, without any training. If you want a real thrill, triple your current income and multiply that by how many more years you'll work.

A Quick Recap

So far we've talked about selling as a profession, talked about why you're in sales and what you want to accomplish. We also looked at the incredible potential for anyone who *chooses* to turn pro.

Next Let's Look At
Your Buyers In Today's Market

The more you understand about your buyers in general, the easier it is to plan your long term success. As you develop your *core selling skills*, you'll also learn through proper questioning to completely understand the buyer who is standing in front of you, so you know exactly how to deliver them their new vehicle today.

So, let's look at your buyers in today's market...

- who they are
- what they really want
- how they make a buying decision
- how we treat them on average
- how easy or tough they are to close
- why price is not most important to them
- how they really make their pricing decisions

Take the time to really understand your buyers, and you'll know how to give them what they want, and avoid making mistakes with them that will cost you sales and income.

"Our 6 salespeople are selling 115.5 units with JVTN®."

"Joe, thanks to you and your virtual training on JVTN® on selling to today's customers, in just six months, all six of our salespeople have improved by over 5 units per month. They each have a rolling 90-day current average of more than 15 units per salesperson.

Your daily training online on JVTN® helps our guys stay sharp with their closing skills, and shows them how to present and demonstrate the vehicle that fits closest to their customer's wants and needs.

Now our 90 day average is 115.5 units per month for the dealership, with just 6 salespeople. Thanks, again!"

– John, General Manager, Chrysler Jeep, Indiana

"Listen to the whispers of your mind.
They're telling you the choices that will help you the most."

– Choices

CHAPTER 4

The Buying Process
And The Selling Process

When we first start selling cars, almost all of us have a ton of enthusiasm. We also have empathy for the customer because we clearly remember what it was like; how excited they get, but also how fearful they are about buying a car.

To start earning those big bucks in sales – I need you to slow down and mentally step back over the curb in this chapter so you can remember what your customers go through to make that *buying* decision. If you will, then I can show you exactly what you need to do to help your customers through the process.

That means you'll sell more cars!

The Buying And Selling Process

Have you ever gone out to buy something expensive like a stereo, furniture or that giant Big Screen TV that you wanted and needed, found the store that had it, *but then ended up <u>not buying</u> because you didn't like the salesperson you talked to?* Of course, we all have, because no matter how badly we want it, or how much we need the product, most of us just refuse to spend big money with people we don't like very much.

On the other hand, have you ever gone out with no intentions of buying and started looking at something expensive, and then ran into a salesperson you did like who gave you a good presentation, built value and before you knew it – you ended up buying that expensive product on the spot? Sure, who hasn't!

Buying a vehicle is a big deal to almost everyone.

In case you forgot; buying a 60" Big Screen TV doesn't even come close in comparison to buying a vehicle. Buying a vehicle is the second largest investment most of us will ever make. And in our lifetimes, most of us will spend way more on the vehicles in our families than we will for our housing.

What does transportation cost a family?

The average person will be buying about 15 vehicles (the average family will purchase 36 vehicles). So if you figure each vehicle will only cost $23,000 (today's pricing), that's still $345,000 each person will spend *before* you count gas, maintenance and insurance in their lifetime on buying a vehicle.

Fuel: At a very low guesstimate of $150 per month for gas per vehicle, driving cars for 50 years will mean another $90,000 out the tailpipe that each of those 3 family members will spend.

Maintenance & Insurance: Add on $1,000 per year in maintenance and insurance for another $50,000. That all adds up to $485,000 each person will spend *in today's dollars*. Depending on where you live, that's as much as buying 2 or 3 houses. Homes don't cost more, cars do. Plus, houses appreciate – cars depreciate.

Let that sink in, and then step back...

Now try to step back to the other side of the curb and think about what an important decision this really is to your prospect. And remember how important *you* are to them in making the decision to purchase your product, at your dealership, from you *today!*

Remember – You're Selling Three Things

If you were just selling a car and nobody had one like yours, and customers had no options on pricing, this would be a piece of cake and you'd make a ton. Oops! No, actually you wouldn't make much money at all. Why? Because if it was that easy, you'd get $7.75 per hour and stand on the showroom floor with a clipboard in your hand trying not to mess up an order.

Because it isn't that simple, you have to sell 3 things...

1. You – both *you* as a person and *you* as a salesperson. As we just covered, if they like you, you'll have an advantage in making the sale. If they don't like you – good luck, you'll need it.

2. Your Product & Your Dealership. Of course you have to sell your product, just remember there is a dealership down the street in almost every town in North America offering the exact same product. They have to see the benefit in buying your product, *from you at your dealership.*

3. The Transaction. This becomes the sticky part. We'll talk about price soon, so I don't want to get ahead of myself; but offering the cheapest pricing in town won't win you many sales. This negotiation process has to be value based, it needs to be swift, it has to be professional, and it has to end with them feeling good about their purchase.

    Again, this process isn't about price. Once we explain that in our Closing & Negotiation class for salespeople, and in our Desking & Negotiation class for managers and teach how to make this a simple 3-Pass Process – it's, "Wow, I had no idea how easy this could be!"

The Buying Process

There are 3 stages to buying an expensive product we all go through. 'Liking' the salesperson is critical, and 71% of the people said they bought because they did. We all make that decision within 3 to 5 minutes of meeting a salesperson. If our first impression is good, we drop our resistance and begin to listen with an open mind. If their presentation makes sense, we consider buying their product. 'Like' is critical, but doesn't guarantee a sale, it just makes a sale possible.

The buying process looks like this...

The Selling Process

Logically, if those are the steps *above* your prospect has to go through to make their decision to purchase from you today, then you need a corresponding step-by-step process *below* to make it happen.

Here's what the selling process looks like...

We developed The New Basics™ so you can close more sales with higher gross profit at 100% customer satisfaction. Following each step exactly takes them from the curb (and not liking, knowing or trusting you) through the Warm Up, Value Building and Closing Phases to get that first set of commitments to own your product.

What's the biggest improvement in following the steps to The New Basics™? To customers, everything they always wanted. To you, about twice as many sales, with close to three times the income you're earning now.

Speed Kills Sales!

We spend two days in our "How To Sell A Car & Close The Sale Today" class teaching The New Basics™ and all of the related skills you need to follow every time you have a prospect on the lot. So there's no way possible to cover all of that in here.

But if you'll take the time to read this chapter again and again, you'll really start to grasp how critical the selling process is and how it, and the buying process have to work together. In fact, just by understanding the two, you'll start making changes in how you sell, and you'll start seeing results immediately.

> *One of the most important points to understand is that...*
> *You cannot speed up this process!*

Your first goal in the process is to help people feel at ease with you, and that takes time. That's why you make a great first impression by looking, acting and sounding like a professional as you greet them. Then you build rapport as you investigate to find their *hot buttons* (what's most important to them on this vehicle they came to buy).

In class we show you how to go through the first six steps in your "Wander-Around" while you're still on the lot. After you've built rapport, found their hot buttons, sold them on your dealership, and especially service – and selected the correct vehicle based on their needs (not price), it's time for your demonstration first and then your first formal walk-around presentation to the secondary driver and then your presentation and demo to the primary driver.

Since the demonstration is the highest emotional state in the buying process, and because you've selected the correct vehicle – at the end of your demo, it's time to start your closing sequence. You'll start with a summary close, then an assumptive close as you pull back on the lot, then you'll get another 10 or 12 buying commitments with your action closes, and wrap it up and head inside with a simple question, that I guarantee they will answer correctly.

And the best part – nothing I described above is about price, not even your closing question. But when you head inside, you'll have the most solid commitment to own you've ever had before.

From what you've read so far...

If you really applied what you know now, and went to 'work to work' every single day – how many more units could you be selling right now?

I could sell _____ more units per month
just by using what I know, and by doing
my very best every day.

"I sold 25 units in 18 days – 9 in one weekend!"

"Joe, after attending your How To Sell A Car Today course I had my best month ever. I was able to sell 25 cars in 18 days, 9 in just one weekend.

What was my secret? Not talking price, investigating, and building value in the cars and our dealership.

Thanks to you and all of your trainers for teaching us how to sell the right way!"

– Simon, Salesperson, U.S.

CHAPTER 5

Selling To Today's Buyer

A Dozen Facts You Need To Know

Play Your Best Odds!

If you were going to gamble in Las Vegas and saw two tables with the exact same game, but one table offered you a 10% chance of winning and the other table offered you a 50% or higher chance of winning each time instead, *which table would you play?*

Of course, any logical person who knew the odds, would play the best odds of winning, especially when the game is the same. *And that's your edge selling cars, too.*

Because there are so many statistics that point you to that "winning table" in sales, you can take the guesswork out of selling and know exactly what to do with each prospect to sell them the vehicle.

Just The Facts

As we go through the *known and proven statistics* in our business, I'll give you a short explanation of what they mean to you and how you can use this knowledge to sell a car today, and to continue to grow every year in sales.

If you've been to our classes anytime over the last 25 years or used any of our training or materials, you'll find that most of these statistics are still almost the same as 10 or 15 years ago. In fact, they've been almost the same since I started selling cars, too.

That statement begs the question: *How can the statistics be the same, especially with all the recent changes in our industry?*

Well, the answer isn't one of those unsolved mysteries – the reasons are actually pretty simple. Most of the statistics are about *people* and *how people buy expensive products,* and those core wants, needs and concerns haven't changed in thousands of years.

The differences today are related to the recession. Prospects are...
More Fearful – More Cautious
More Informed – More Demanding

Today's buyers have changed in ways that affect their purchasing. In the last few years almost every consumer, buying any type of product has become more fearful, more cautious, more demanding. And with Internet access, they're armed with more information about the product than ever before.

In the old days (2007) when people were yanking money out of their home equity to buy cars, so many people in our business developed the habit and belief that they 'could just show up for work selling cars, and because everybody was buying cars in record numbers, that they'd make money in spite of what they really knew about selling'. And in fact – that was true.

Until the recession hit, you really didn't have to develop your skills or build your business to make decent money. You could go to work, wait for an 'up', and earn $42,000 per year in spite of your skills.

Earlier in this book when I was telling 'my story', I said when I finally learned to sell, it was from the most successful people in history like Napoleon Hill, W. Clement Stone, Ben Franklin and Socrates. Those guys understood the principles that drive all human behavior and in one way or another, they all said:

> *Selling isn't really about product and it isn't about price. It's about people and it's about value, and whether the sale is made or lost, depends on your persuasion skills.*

Yeah, I know, that's a bold statement, or at least it is until you analyze this next critical point:

> *80% of your buyers and competitors will continue to do what they always do. And that's to your advantage if you turn pro in sales.*

Prospects: 80% of your prospects will continue to buy the way people buy; they will search to find a salesperson they *like*, they will resist until they see the *value*, and then with your assistance to help them make a decision (closing), they'll *purchase* the product.

Competition: 80% of the dealers, managers and salespeople in your market will keep doing what they do, too, and that's a 'lousy job'.

They'll *wish* for an ad or event they *hope* will fill the lot with buyers. They'll *beg* the manufacturer to send them only the hottest models their prospects want to *buy.* The managers will continue to focus their advertising, their marketing, their website, their events, their salespeople and their negotiation on *price.* And you can rest assured the salespeople down the street will *continue to take every shortcut* they can, if your prospect stops there first.

Here's the real advantage pros in sales have…

> *You aren't competing with the dealership down the street or with their pricing. You're only competing with the salesperson your prospect will talk to at the dealership down the street.*

That under-trained, poorly managed and most likely unmotivated salesperson will take every shortcut possible when they're dealing with the prospects they talk to, because they haven't been taught to sell and because their managers haven't been taught to manage.

A Sales Professional Has No Competition!

Here's one final tip on the stats I'll cover...

Like many of you reading this, I was the 8-car guy with a list a mile long on why I wasn't selling more cars. And when I first read these statistics, I said...

"No way, I just can't believe this is all true."

Even though I didn't want to believe, I knew the stats were true because I'd found them stated in so many different, reliable places.

Change your attitude and your habits...

Habits and attitudes are hard to break and I knew I had my work cut out for me on changing my mind on these stats. When I started selling cars again I wasn't seeing just buyers. I was *still seeing* 'lookers', 'shoppers' and 'flaky looking people' who didn't look like they could afford the steering wheel, much less the whole car.

> *Before I could change my results in sales, first I had to change my mind. And I knew the quicker that I honestly bought into these stats, the sooner I'd sell more cars.*

So I wrote out the statistics we're going to cover on 3 x 5 cards, and I carried them around in my pocket for a couple of months and read them a dozen times each day, *until I believed them completely*.

And then it happened!

After reading these statistics again and again, day after day, I really stopped seeing lookers, shoppers and people who couldn't buy. All I could see were buyers, and they were everywhere. If you want to grow and improve and close more sales, that's your first step, too.

The easiest way to double your sales overnight is to believe the statistics, assume everyone is on the lot to buy, and just start giving *everyone* your most enthusiastic and your very best value building presentation and demonstration. You have zero to lose and everything to gain – so why not go for the gold?

> *If you will – you'll definitely sell more cars, have more fun and make more money!*

The Quick Facts: A Baker's Dozen

About your prospects...

1. **99% of the people want to drive the vehicle before they buy it.**

   That's the funny thing about buying expensive products; people really do want to see how they work before they'll part with their cash (or credit).

   I doubt that many of you reading this bought your big screen TV without seeing one turned on first, and you probably didn't buy your sofa without sitting on it first. Because those statements are most likely true, you need to realize and admit that other people don't buy cars and trucks (that cost even more) without driving them first, either.

   Skipping the demo is one of the costliest mistakes salespeople make and it's one of the first shortcuts most salespeople *hope* to be able to take when they're trying to sell their product.

   Why is it a mistake? The 99% stat itself says it all, so read it again; people want to drive it *before* they buy it. Why try to win by skipping a demo and having just a 1% chance of making the sale, when there's a 99% chance you'll lose?

   Even more important; when people are driving the vehicle, they hit the highest emotional point in the sale and are taking mental ownership of your product. To you, that means the final lap of the demonstration is when you want to close the sale. Get to class or train on JVTN® and I'll teach you *exactly* when to start closing, *exactly* what to say and *exactly* how to use the demonstration to double your deliveries.

   Of course I know some people will tell you they don't need to drive it and just want to know your best pricing. Tip: Listen to that little voice in your head. It will remind you that if you fall for what they just said, you'll lose the sale. It's just a fact that if they don't drive it *before* you get into pricing, down, trades or payments, you'll miss the sale almost every time. Even if you make a sale, you'll leave almost all of the gross on the table.

The average salesperson in our industry really fights the system on this, and only gives 3 or 4 out of every 10 prospects a *good* presentation and demonstration – and the average salesperson delivers just 10 units. ('Good' is the key word.)

If you want to sell a car today – play these best odds...

50% of the people buy on the spot (stat #10) when they get what they feel is a good presentation and a good demonstration of your product. That means one of the easiest ways to close more sales is to just play the odds and give everyone you possibly can your very best presentation and demonstration. Let the numbers start working in your favor.

We also do training with the largest boat, and RV dealers and manufacturers in North America. And if you sell those products, getting people behind the wheel before you ask for the order will have a tremendous impact not only on your sales volume, but also on your gross profit.

And yes, we all know it's more trouble to demo a 40' coach or a boat, that isn't the question. The only question is, will you *choose* to go to the trouble to demonstrate your product with more of your prospects so you can increase your sales volume?

A demonstration is also more than a test drive. A demo is required for more complex systems on vehicles these days; navigation, joy sticks, computers, and even how to set the A/C and tune a radio has gone from a no-brainer to a 20 page manual.

Plus, if you're selling boats or RVs, you have electrical, air conditioning, leveling, slide outs, electronics, even more sophisticated navigation, disposal and other systems. You have to demonstrate those, too, so your prospects can see how easy it is to operate and so they can take *mental ownership*.

To become a pro – learn how to count. Average salespeople count failures, pros count successes. 8-car guys count *how often things don't work* (like demos & prospecting calls), to justify why they don't do it. Pros count how often things *do work,* so they know how many demos or calls it takes to sell more.

---

2.   **78% of the people who go out and look at a vehicle – buy one.**

That little dot at the end of that sentence is a *period*. That means this statistic is not open for debate and you can forget what the huddle says about this stat being incorrect.

Even better news, these are Hot Prospects because...

• 38% buy within 4 hours of stopping at the first dealership,

• 57% buy within 3 days, and

• 90% buy within a week.

So if you're looking for a sale, don't worry about which person on the lot is a buyer, because there's an 8 out of 10 chance the one you're with *will buy* and a 50/50 chance they'll buy from you today, if you do your job right.

More good news: 85% of the people said their salesperson didn't build rapport and didn't investigate before they tried to sell them something, and 88% said they got a poor presentation and a poor demonstration.

Why is that good news for you?

Because if a prospect tells you they've been shopping, that's what happened while they were at that dealership down the street. Remember the facts: Your competition (that below average, under-trained, unmotivated salesperson down the street) didn't build any rapport, didn't investigate, and gave them a lousy presentation and demonstration. Now just do your job, avoid price, build value, and collect a commission.

Note: If you really are doing your best to doubt the statistics I covered above – step up and prove them right or wrong.

It's easy, just get every person's name, address and phone number who doesn't buy from you for two weeks. Then wait 7 days to contact them and when you do, you'll find that 78% have already bought – just not from you.

No mystery here – just do your job and you'll close more sales!

3. **85% decided to buy a vehicle before they ever left home.**

They really aren't 'just looking,' they say that out of habit, just like you do when you walk up to a salesperson.

Realistically, they won't just walk up to a stranger (you) and say, "If you do a great job of making me *like* and *trust* you; if you find *my driving wants and needs* and then if you do a great job *presenting and demonstrating* your product; and if you *build the value* to me of owning so it's much higher than the price so I can feel good about making my decision to purchase, I'm ready to buy a vehicle today, from you."

They never say it, but that's exactly what you have
to accomplish with every prospect who walks on the lot.

4. **58% buy the same product they went to look at first.**

If 78% who walk on the lot buy within a week, if over 90% of the prospects who buy have been on the Internet checking things out, and if 85% decided to buy a vehicle before they even left home, if you sell Fords and they show up at your Ford store first…I think it's pretty safe to say that they're not only considering buying a Ford, but they're also willing to buy it from your dealership and from you today, if you'll just take the time to do your job right.

Seriously – just how hard should it be
to sell somebody something who came to buy?

"Units are up 27% and gross is up 58%."

"Our units increased 27% over the last 12 months, and our gross is up 58% from your Sales and Management training daily on JVTN® and your other materials. I estimate your training has given me a 20-to-1 return on my investment and I've also dramatically decreased my advertising budget. It's been a great year, and only getting better." *– George, Ford Dealer*

Congratulations to George and his team!

5. **71% buy because they like you, trust you and respect you.**

    Ben Franklin and Socrates both talked about how important
    the relationship (rapport) is between the salesperson and the
    buyer. It was true then and it's true now, because you and I
    react the exact same way. If people like you, you'll have a good
    chance of making the sale. If they don't like you – again, good
    luck because you'll need it.

    The New Basics™ we teach are designed with one simple result
    in mind; take a stranger who doesn't like you, know you or
    trust you through the process of buying (and selling) so you
    finish up at the other end with a sale and almost double the
    gross profit you're getting now. And it works! So why argue
    with a proven process that will make you more money?

    ----

    *"Joe, I have been in the car business for 25 years. For the last
    four months I've been training on JVTN® and my attitude has
    skyrocketed; I go to work to work and by going back to the Basics,
    staying off price, greeting the prospect properly and building
    rapport, my average gross per unit has gone from $1,200 to
    $3,000. I train everyday on JVTN®."*   *– Nick, SP, Buick*

    Tripling your income is great – congratulations, Nick!

6. **90+% of the decisions to purchase will be influenced by the
    woman in the group (or at home). Plus, over 50% of the vehicles
    delivered, are delivered to women.**

    Quick check: If you're a guy and if you really aren't sure how
    much women influence the decisions we (men) make, just go
    ask your wife or girlfriend or mom or your sister. And if you
    can't reach one of them, just ask the next woman you talk to.

    A friend of ours wanted to buy herself a new SUV. She took
    her husband with her, not to help her buy it or to help her
    make a decision. She just took him because he's her husband
    and that's what most married couples do.

At the first dealership, she asked the salesperson a few questions and the salesperson spoke to her husband when he answered her questions. She didn't really like being ignored, especially since she was the buyer, so they left.

They went to another dealership, and she asked the salesperson a few questions. Same thing, he talked to her husband instead of her, so they left again.

Third dealership; she asked questions, the salesperson responded to her, still acknowledging her husband as he should, and to cut the story short, she pulled out their checkbook and bought the vehicle.

I used to make a ton of sales to women and kids by doing the same thing. Dozens of parents said, "Thank you for spending time with our son (or daughter), nobody else did," as they took delivery. And women buyers really get tired of the 'where's your husband?' attitude from most salespeople.

Our business is so behind the times in selling to women and in hiring women in sales and sales management, it's crazy. Do the job you're supposed to be doing with every person on the lot (man, woman or kid on a bicycle). You'll definitely increase your sales overnight to women, but you'll also increase sales overall to everyone, because you'll be in the habit of doing a great job all of the time – not just some of the time.

"Before using JVTN®, I was averaging 8 units a month, now I'm averaging 16 per month. After completing the very energetic 'Fast Start for Salespeople' Series, I'm more organized, more effective with my follow-up, and building my own customer base so I don't have to wait for an 'up' anymore. JVTN® is a great training program and I can't wait to go to class."
– Kathy, Salesperson, Ford

Double units and income is great – Congratulations, Kathy!

7. **30% of the people have a *family member* who will be buying a new or used vehicle within the next 90 days. And 62% *know someone* who will be buying within 90 days.**

   There are tons of 'get rich quick' schemes and people fall for them every day. Here's a get rich method that works like a charm and it's like pulling teeth to get salespeople to do it. It's called prospecting and follow-up.

   We'll blame salespeople's *lack of enthusiasm* for doing follow-up and for prospecting on a *lack of education* up to this point, though. It's hard to do anything if you don't see the benefit and if you don't know how to do it properly and effectively.

   Carl Sewell, the Dallas car dealer, wrote a book called "Customers For Life" on the value to dealerships of retaining customers forever. After I really understood these stats and learned how to sell professionally...

   I wanted to be my customer's salesperson for life!

   Why is learning to prospect (and follow-up) so critical to your success? It's just a math problem. Average families will purchase about 36 vehicles in their lifetimes.

   With that many potential sales to every family, learning how to stay in touch so you can retain each customer seems like another one of those no-brainer things to do.

   It's easy to show you how to double your sales by focusing on the steps to selling, closing sales and on immediately following up with the people who don't buy, so you can get them back in right away for another shot at making the sale.

   We can show you how to double sales again and keep your income growing forever by developing your retention skills: Follow-Up, Prospecting, Referral Prospecting, Building Your Master List and developing your Phone Skills. These skills help you sell more vehicles today, and help you keep building your business, year after year. So get to class and get your dealer to sign you and the other salespeople up for JVTN® because these are your career-building skills.

"From $40,000 to $75,000 after class."

"Before attending your course I was earning around $40,000 per year. This year I'm on track to reach $75,000. I learned how important effective follow-up is and now I'm working with more referrals. Thanks, Joe." Jamaal, Salesperson, Ford

Great job, Jamaal. Double income – Congratulations!

**Now let's look at some of the facts
about their buying motives and decisions...**

8. **20% of the features on your vehicle – that's all your prospects care about, *not* everything you know about your product.**

    How many of you know a nice, very likeable, walking, talking, product knowledge expert who knows everything and sells almost nothing? Sure, we all know a few.

    Product experts are certainly nice people and hard workers and they are a serious benefit to our industry. The manufacturers, your dealer and managers and I as a trainer, all recommend you learn *everything* you can about your product.

    But if product knowledge is critical and if these product experts know everything there is to know about the product, then why aren't they usually selling more units?

    Two reasons…

    1. They tell every prospect *everything* they know.
    2. Prospects don't care about *everything* they know.

    Every prospect has Hot Buttons, and those are their own personal reasons they want a particular product. For instance, they like the looks, they need the storage, they need 3rd row seating for the kids, they need the towing capacity, they want the better mileage, they want those 38 air bags to protect them, and just about anything else you can think of.

That also means they have Cold Buttons, and those are the things they just don't care very much about. If their Hot Button is Comfort and Convenience and you spend your presentation talking about their Cold Buttons; Performance and Economy, you're dead in the water.

Don't misunderstand, it isn't that they don't want those other benefits; it's just that they don't get them as excited as their Hot Buttons do. Your goal is to get people as excited as you can about owning your product, not bore them off the lot.

If you talk about a bunch of features they don't really care about, you either lose their attention completely, or they hear the cash register ticking higher and higher on things they don't want but know they'll have to pay for.

Cover a Hot Button, move closer to the sale...

Sales psychologists have studied people in sales situations and found that every time you talk about a feature people care about, a Hot Button, you move a step forward in the sale. On the other hand, every time you talk about a feature they don't care about, at best you stand still, but more often you take several steps backwards in the sale.

Too many salespeople talk themselves into a sale and back out of one, if they aren't careful.

I learned this accidentally. I was watching another salesperson getting ready to write-up a prospect on one of those big old *long* Chrysler Imperials. The salesperson just couldn't stop telling the customer what he knew, and he said, "It's __ feet __ inches long." The prospect stopped dead in his tracks and said, "I don't know if that will fit in my garage, I need to go check first." Whether it fit in his garage or not, that was reason enough for him to leave and he never came back.

Tip: Once you have a commitment to purchase, stop covering features on the vehicle and start getting more commitments to own. I'll show you exactly how to do this in Closing the Sale in The New Basics™ on JVTN® or in our classes.

9. **80% of the buying (and selling) is done in your (4) presentation steps of the sale.**

Read the stat in (#8) again on prospects being interested in just 20% of the features on your vehicles. Now add presenting, demonstrating and closing to the equation.

Once you discover their Hot Buttons, your presentation specifically focuses on the features they care about, the advantages to them of having those features and the benefits to them of owning the features and your product. (FABs for short.)

Great feature, advantage and benefit selling, mixed with great closing skills and the ability to overcome objections equals one lean, mean closing machine in sales. Any salesperson can learn how to close, even if you don't have that 'mean' look about you.

"After class I've doubled my sales from 6 to 13 and my commissions went from $150 per unit to $534. Thanks for showing me the professional way to sell cars and make money." Chris, Salesperson

I did some quick math on Chris' improvement…
Was…6 units x $150 per unit = $900
Now…13 units x $534 per unit = $6,942
Wow! Congratulations, Chris!

10. **50% of the people buy on the spot when they get what they feel is a good presentation and a good demonstration of the product.**

Remember that 2 or 3-car day you had a few months ago? Remember how much fun you were having and how easy you made it for the prospects to have fun, too?

Statistically, since 78% will be buying, if you only talked to 38 people on the lot, 30 are buyers. Since you could close 50% of those 30 buyers – that means you could deliver 15 of the 38 people you talk to, if you'll just treat every prospect like a buyer.

No pre-qualifying, just great rapport and investigation, killer targeted presentations, well-planned demos that build emotions, and solid closes and objection methods to wrap it all up.

If you think about it, that sure sounds a lot easier than talking to 75-100 people every month instead, pre-qualifying most of them, focusing everything on price, only giving a few presentations, even fewer demonstrations, grinding out deals for hours at a time and selling just 8 units every month.

"Joe, I was averaging just 8 units per month and right after your class I delivered 13 units that week!" DW, SP, Dodge / Chrysler

WOW – doubled your income the next week! Great job!

DW just went back with new skills, a renewed attitude and really did her job with enthusiasm. If you'll do the same thing, you will close more sales and deliver more units today!

11. **86% of the people buy a different make or model, or a different color or with different features, than they planned to purchase.**

When they ask, "Do you have a white one?" and you respond with, "No, but I can get you one," it costs you sales!

Why? A couple of reasons. Remember when your prospects said, "We want white," and as you were walking the lot to find that car, they passed a blue one and said, "That's a pretty nice color, too," then two minutes later they saw the red one and said, "Wow, we hadn't seen this before, we like it," and then they ended up driving away in the pre-owned, black pick-up truck because it's the one they really needed, and it fit neatly in their budget!

Hardly anybody (only 14%) drives away in *what they said* they wanted. No, not because we switched them to something they didn't like. They switched because they can cruise the Internet and their friends can show them their cars, and they can think they want that white car with a sunroof and 22" wheels. But a lot of things happen once they're around all those other *choices* on your lot, and even more things happen when it gets down to the money it takes to buy that perfect vehicle.

Most people are *impulse buyers* to a point, so they end up with a different color, with different equipment. Plus, since only 58% bought the same product they looked at first (usually their first choice since they stopped there first), that means 42% don't even buy the same brand they intended to purchase!

I want white, do you have one?

- To lose the sale, respond with: "No, but I can get you one."

- To make a sale, respond with: "Let's go see (bypass color) who's the lucky one Bob, is the new car for you or Betty?" (As you start walking toward the lot).

"I more than doubled my unit sales (from 8 to 17) and doubled my gross per unit after your Sales Class! Having those extra closes from class worked." – Dave, Salesperson, Ford

Wow – a double, double. Congratulations, Dave!

12. **96% of the people who are given figures on the lot or in the office and who leave without buying – shop those figures. It's the same percentage with prices on the phone and Internet.**

No matter what you've experienced or been told by the smartest 6-car guy, and no matter what you've been *conditioned* to believe by getting beaten up over price so often; price is *not* the most important decision people make.

Price is #16 on people's list of buying motives. Remember those other things they say: "We want white with a sunroof, we need third row seating for the kids, we live in the desert and need rear air, we want the double rear doors, flush fold seats, we need the navigation system, we want the rear entertainment system, we want 22" wheels and we want your best price."

Price is important to them, but you can bet that they aren't going to leave a couple of the kids at home in the desert just because you have a 5-passenger vehicle that's cheaper.

Drop the price – drop the value!

When you say, "We can save you at least $3,500 on this," what your prospect heard you say was…

"This vehicle never was worth the $43,500 we were asking for it, so we'll start at $40,000 and work our way down from there."

When you start dropping your price, if you didn't have a price shopper before, you just created one, and it will usually cost you a sale – and talking price always costs you gross.

This isn't rocket science. When you drop the price, they lose confidence that they're making a good 'price' buying decision. Now they're confused, so they have to shop around to make sure they aren't paying too much (in their minds).

Plus when you focus everything on price, you will logically lose sales, because you can't go low enough to make some of those deals. Even when you do make the sale, since it was price focused, that means the grosses are so low it almost doesn't matter, anyway. Other than a unit count, there's nothing left.

Did I mention 3,355 salespeople responded to our online survey, and salespeople who attend our workshops and use JVTN®, *earn more than twice as much as those who don't?*

Why? Because in class and on JVTN®, we teach you how to properly handle price questions, concerns and objections you get on the lot, so you can build value and close the sale on owning the vehicle, not on how cheap you can sell it.

Almost any dealership can beat you on *cheap*,
but hardly any of them can even come close on *value*.

`` ---------------

"Joe, after your Sales School I had my best month ever. I went from 11 units per month to 20 the next month and my income jumped from $3,500 per month to $15,500. Now I stay off price on the lot and have more skills and confidence." Chad, Salesperson

Wow – from $42,000 to $186,000 if Chad just keeps it up!

13. **33% of the people who leave a dealership without buying will come back with good follow-up, and when they do, 67% buy.**

It's too bad we don't follow-up with everyone, because 33% of them (1 out of 3) will come back with good follow-up, and 67% of them (7 out of 10) buy the vehicle on that second visit.

There are a lot more statistics like these you really need to understand. There are so many more opportunities to sell, and we cover dozens more of these facts in class and on JVTN®.

One more question real quick...
How would you like to sell 8 more units per month?

Since we're talking about how to move from Average to High Achiever overnight, let's finish up our Baker's Dozen (13) here with the math on the statistics of Unsold Follow-Up.

This book is about your potential in sales. If you will follow-up every person who doesn't buy from you, most people reading this can double their sales and income, overnight.

To find a number we can work with in the example on the next page, let's assume the following:

a. You talk to an average number of people; 3 or 4 per day.

b. You sell 10 units a month; a couple *each week* right now, and on average you earn $300 per unit ($3,000 per month).

c. You also write-up 2 or 3 people each week who don't buy.

That means at least *9 people you talk to each week leave without buying.* So let's look at the math on unsold follow-up with those 9 on the next page...

"I jumped my average from 12 to 21.5 from JVTN®."

"In the last couple of years, I have jumped my average from 12 to 21.5 a month! Watching my JVTN® segments, passing my quizzes and applying what I learned helped me sell over 170 units in just the last 7 months alone. Thanks for making it so easy."
– Craig, Salesperson, Pennsylvania

Potential: Unsold Follow-Up

The Math:		
	9	people a week leave without buying
	x 33%	will come back with good follow-up
	= 3	who come back in to see you
	x 67%	who buy on this 2nd visit
	= 2	additional sales per week
	x 4	weeks per month
	= 8	additional sales per month!
	$2,400	*additional commission*
	+	*extra bonuses for units*

*The end result…*if you do your unsold follow-up, you will go from 10 units to 18 units and at least double your income with more bonuses. Plus, your grosses will go up dramatically if you don't focus on price on the lot or in your follow-up calls.

Instead of using price to get them back in, get to class or go through the 'Unsold Follow-Up' chapters on JVTN® and we'll show you how to create urgency without talking about price.

Then start using the tracking in the VSA® / JVTN® so you can find your own stats. Once you do, just focus on making one or two real improvements each month. If you will – the sky is the limit on your potential in sales.

- Which fact in this chapter surprised you the most?   # ___

  How will you use that to help you sell more? _____

  _____

- Which fact offers <u>you</u> the most potential?   # ___

     Make this homework with a date to complete.

A Baker's Dozen: Key Facts You Want To Internalize

1. 99% of the people want to drive the vehicle before they buy it.

2. 78% of the people who actually take the time to go out and look at a new or used vehicle, end up buying one (soon).

3. 85% of the people who do end up buying, decided to buy before they ever left home – we just helped them.

4. 58% of the people buy the same product they looked at first.

5. 71% of the people bought because they liked, trusted and respected the salesperson they dealt with.

6. 90%+ of the decision to purchase will be influenced by the woman in the group (or at home), and over 50% of the vehicles delivered, are purchased by women.

7. 30% of all the people have a family member who will be trading vehicles within the next 90 days, and 62% of all people know someone who will be trading within 90 days.

8. 20% of the features on your vehicles are all your prospects care about, not everything you know about your product.

9. 80% of the selling (and buying) is done in your four presentation steps of the sale.

10. 50% of the people buy on the spot when they get what they feel is a good presentation and good demonstration of the product.

11. 86% of the people buy a different make or model, or a different color or with different features than they planned to purchase.

12. 96% of the people who are given figures on the lot or in the office, and who leave without buying, shop those figures, and it's the same percentage on the phones and Internet.

13. 90% of the people who leave without buying are never contacted again. That's too bad because with good follow-up, 33% will come back in and 67% will buy.

Tip: Do what I did to change your thinking and habits. Copy this page, carry it with you and read it several times every day for 30 days.

Read these daily and you'll stop pre-qualifying and start giving everyone a great presentation and demonstration; you'll sell more units, hold more gross, get better CSI, have more fun and make a lot more money!

CHAPTER 6

Know The Players

— — —

Closing Ratios Of The

Five Different Types Of Buyers

We don't have just one type of buyer that you'll be selling to in your career in sales. We have five different groups of people who buy from us. One group is usually pretty tough to work with, and the other four groups are easier.

The best part – you get to pick which groups you will focus on selling to the rest of your career. If you make the smarter choice, you'll have a lot of fun selling, and earning over $100,000 every year will be a piece of cake.

The average closing ratio across the board is 20%.
That's the combined average of all five types of prospects.
20% is not the average for any specific group of prospects.

1. Walk-Ins...10% is the average closing ratio for walk-in prospects.

(That means salespeople <u>are not</u> closing 90% of walk-in traffic.)

Can you improve your closing ratios and sell more to walk-ins? Absolutely! *Results* in sales are relative to the quantity and quality of your sales *activities*. To improve the % of people who buy, just improve your selling *activities* that affect your closing ratios.

Remember...
50% of all of the people buy on the spot on average, when they get a good presentation and good demonstration. Because this is a statistic based on average prospects, it includes walk-ins.

But here's another *catch,* the word 'good'. You can't give a *good* presentation or demonstration *if you didn't complete each of the first four steps of The New Basics™ effectively.* (Great 1st Impression, Greet, Rapport, Investigate). You have to get to know each prospect and you have to find out what they want and why they want it, so you know what to focus on in your presentation, demo and closing.

This is what confuses and frustrates the warm and friendly product knowledge experts who don't sell many units. They just can't figure out why they aren't selling more; they know their product inside out, they tell everybody everything there is to know about their product, plus they love people and the car business.

Product knowledge is absolutely critical, and every salesperson needs a lot more than most have right now. But prospects don't care about everything you know – they only care about the things important to them. That's why you have to build rapport and investigate.

Remember: 80% of the selling is done in your presentation steps, on just 20% of the features. To sell more, think *targeted* presentations.

Ask more questions in the first four steps of The New Basics™
to find their Hot Buttons, before you start presenting and demonstrating.

2. **Phone / Internet...50% is the average closing ratio for these prospects when you get them on the lot.**

Read it again – your closing ratio is not 50% on the phone. You close 5 out of 10 that show up on the lot. One of the biggest mistakes salespeople make on incoming sales calls, Internet leads, and outgoing sales calls is they forget that their only goal is to set a firm appointment that shows up on the lot.

The goal is not to try to sell the car on the phone...

You certainly need to be positive, answer general questions and get the prospect excited about coming in to look at the vehicle. But if you don't learn how to get the prospect from the phone and onto your lot, you can't sell them anything.

Follow these steps to set up an appointment that shows...
- Warm and friendly greeting
- Congratulate them and get control with questions
- Get their number first, then their name
- Confirm that you have the vehicle (or can get it)
- Get the appointment with Either / Or questions
- Firm it up on the quarter hour (38% more will show)
- Anchor the appointment and repeat it 3-5 times (correctly)
- Confirm every appointment you *think* you have

There are certainly exceptions, but on most calls, the shorter it is, the more likely you are to see (75%) of them on the lot.

On Internet Leads... The goal is also an appointment. That happens much quicker with a phone call. Most leads include a phone number, so send a quick email through the VSA®, "With a customer – I'll call you soon." Then call them in 2 minutes and stick with the plan above.

Big Misunderstanding On Phone Skills!

Phone skills are not a unique set of skills. Phone skills are just selling skills you use when you're on a call. You control the conversation, build rapport, bypass price, and close on a firm appointment. On the lot you use the same types of questions to control the conversation, build rapport, bypass price and close the sale. Get to class and develop your core skills and these Internet leads and phone calls will be easier.

3. **Referrals...60% is the average closing ratio for referrals, and through prospecting in person or on the phone.**

    Why are closing ratios getting higher as we go?

Selling expensive products is almost always a relationship based process and once you communicate with someone in person, by phone or through the mail or email, you start to develop a relationship. Once that happens, the 'like' part of the buying process carries you through to higher closing ratios.

Think about the 10% closing ratio with walk-ins versus 50% on phone or Internet prospects. Both were strangers, but by the time they show up on the lot, salespeople have already built some rapport with them on the phone or online. They talked awhile or went back and forth in a few emails and now the prospect feels a little more comfortable or they won't show up.

That means if everybody just called in first and you had those 3 minutes of conversation before your prospects walked on the lot, your closing ratio would go from 10% to 50%.

Remember: 71% buy because they like their salesperson.

Here are the two most important facts we are never taught about the real benefits of being in the car business:

30% of all the people have a family member who'll trade vehicles within the next 90 days, and 62% know someone who'll trade.

The car business didn't die – it slowed down and will probably recover completely. Even if business is off 30%, that means 70% of the people are still out buying, and all you have to do is find them.

Most dealers, managers and salespeople who are still down in the dumps about today's market, have forgotten about all the people in their database and community who *are* still buying today.

If you think about it...

- Somebody's lease is expiring right now, today
- Somebody just wrecked their car and needs a replacement
- Somebody has to buy one of their kids a car today
- Somebody spends too much on repairs and will buy today
- Some people will buy today because they can and want to

The Question Is..."Where do you find these prospects?"

That's the benefit of selling cars – just open your eyes. Everybody has a vehicle now, and they'll be getting another one when they're done with this one. Plus, everybody they know also has a vehicle and will eventually trade it in, too.

Referrals aren't usually price shoppers and you have the edge when someone is referred to you. The person who referred them also transferred your credibility, which means you've already started to establish the *relationship* with that referral, before you even meet them.

How do you get referrals and where do you find them?

You have a computer full of prospects, and you can quickly sit down and make a list of everyone else you know or deal with at the grocery store, gas station, laundry, etc. Remember – 30% have a family member who'll be buying in 90 days, and 62% know someone who will.

• How long does a 3 to 5 minute prospecting call take? *3-5 minutes.*
• How many of those calls could you make each day? *10-20 easily!*
• What would that be worth? *About 10 extra sales each month.*

Service Customers close at 60% – almost as high as repeats.

Do this: Count the steps from your showroom floor to your service drive. That's how far you are from a gold mine. Why? Because 30% are buyers within 90 days, and 8 out of 10 service customers would buy at your dealership. They're comfortable, they just need a salesperson.

Unfortunately, 80% of sales never make it to service and more than 80% of service customers never make it back to the sales department.

The service department is one of your best sources for business. It's convenient, and best of all, when you do bring a customer up front, they aren't shopping. They haven't been online or down the street to compare products, and they aren't price focused. They're easier to close and your gross profit and commissions skyrocket.

Just make it a goal to *wander* out to service and strike up a conversation with a minimum of 5 people each day. Use the referral script when you can and you'll deliver at least 5 more units per month.

Orphan owners at 60% closing ratio

90% of the sold customers are never contacted again about buying another vehicle. Since 95% of your own customers *and* the dealership's previous customers, will all buy more vehicles – your orphan owner database is a gold mine. Use the same script, just a slightly different focus on the call. See either JVTN® series: Follow-Up & Prospect, or Build Your Business By Phone for exactly what to say.

Also see your manager or the GM or Dealer and ask for permission to start turning those orphan owners in the database back into valuable customers who spend money in every department. It benefits you both; you earn more commissions and the dealership increases their sales.

Friends, acquaintances, and people you deal with every day at 60%+

Don't you hate it when you find out that a friend, a neighbor, the kid at the pizza place, the couple at church, or the counter person at your dry cleaners tells you about the new car they just got – that they didn't buy from you?

When you do find out, it's always the poor me, sad face and, "How come you didn't see me?" Reply: "I forgot (didn't know) you sold cars."

There's gold in your service drive, in the customer base and with all of the people you deal with outside the dealership. But like the big Gold Rush in California back in the 1800s we talked about, not everybody grabbed a shovel and headed west. Back then, just like with most salespeople now, people can explain why...

> "It's too much trouble."
>
> "I'm too busy."
>
> "I don't have time."
>
> "It doesn't work."
>
> "I might miss an up."
>
> "I just don't want to."

Learning to build your own business and working with friendly people turns a hard job into a very enjoyable, high paying profession.

4. **Unsold Prospects...67% is the average closing ratio for unsold prospects (be-backs) you bring back into your dealership.**

   (Closing the sale with 'be-backs' is 6.7 times easier than closing the sale the first time they were on the lot. Such a deal!)

HOT – HOT – HOT

You talk about wanting a hot prospect – the people you didn't sell a vehicle to are the hottest prospects you have in your system.

If you'll remember those "Baker's Dozen Stats", there's a...

- 78% probability they're a buyer
- 38% chance they'll buy within the next 4 hours
- 57% chance they'll buy within 3 days
- 90% chance they'll be burning gas within a week in their new (or used) vehicle – hopefully from you
- 33% chance they'll come back to see you with good follow-up
- 67% chance they'll buy on the spot on their second visit

Other than a repeat customer you bring back in, no other group is this easy to close. Not only that, you've probably already done 95% of the work to sell this prospect. You've already spent 1 to 2 hours with them, and when they come back in, it's usually a very fast process. *Who could ask for anything more?*

I forgot, how long does that 3 to 5-minute follow-up call take?

About 3-5 minutes. And remember, the goal with the unsold prospect is just to get a firm appointment that shows. You aren't calling to educate them on pricing or product or to try to work a deal over the phone; the only goal is to *set an appointment that shows.*

The worst follow-up call you can make is...

   "Hi Bob, this is Joe down at the dealership – have you guys given any more thought to getting a car?"

Stop opening with that question unless you don't mind hearing, "We decided to hold off a while."

With the VSA®, you have scripts in the system you can read until you master them, and training on JVTN® to continually improve sales.

5. **Repeat Customers…70% is the average closing ratio for a previous customer you bring back through follow-up.**

We work with half of the top 500 dealers in the US, half the top Internet dealers and 3,500 of the other most motivated dealers of every size – and some of the highest achievers in sales in the world.

All of those top dealerships, dealer groups and top salespeople have one thing in common; they focus on building their business.

A dealer who builds their repeat business lowers their cost per sale by two thirds and will net 3 to 5 times more than a dealer selling the exact same number of units at the exact same gross, who depends on a huge ad budget to draw a (tough) crowd of walk-ins.

The highest achievers I know in sales also focus on their repeat and referral business. All of the 30, 40 and 50-car a month salespeople I know do the majority of their sales with these types of customers.

In fact, it would be virtually impossible for a salesperson who only closes 10% of the prospects they talk to on the lot – to sustain a 40 unit average with just floor traffic. They'd need 400 people on the lot every month to deliver those 40 units. Even if they got much better and closed 30% of all the people they talk to, for them to deliver 40 units, they'd still have to talk to 133 people on the lot each month.

High achievers spend less time in the dealership. Not only do the highest achievers sell a ton of units and make the most money, most of them spend less time in the dealership than average and above average salespeople who depend on floor traffic. They come to work, say 'Hi' to old friends all day and deliver vehicles.

Added benefit: The gross profit on repeat and referrals is 40% higher.

If you're closing 20% of your prospects now; to sell 15 units to walk-ins, you'll need to talk to 75 people on the lot, mostly price shopping strangers. If you average $400 per sale in commission and bonuses, that's $6,000+ per month which is a great income, no question.

But what if you did all your business with repeat customers? With a 70% closing ratio, to sell 15, you'd only need to put 22 people on the lot each month, and you'd make 40% more – $8,400 total.

Friendly people – almost no grind – and you'd earn $100,000+ per year selling 15 units per month...just from following a daily process that includes those 5-minute phone calls to keep 'em coming back.

Repeat business, referrals, service customers, orphan owners, incoming sales calls, Internet leads and be-backs – are your ticket to $100,000 and more every year. You make it happen by developing your 'Business Development' skills and learning how to generate your own business instead of wasting a day hoping for a decent 'up'.

We teach salespeople how to build their customer base and this is why the survey pointed out salespeople who go through our training *earn $60,000 more* each year than those who don't use our training to develop their skills and learn to plan their future.

The next time you pass a dealership, drive slow or park across the street for a few minutes and just watch the salespeople. They're probably good people but they're just hoping to make money.

Instead of learning more and coming to work to work, they settled for hanging around waiting for their dealer to supply them with an 'up' and hopefully a sale. What they get instead is a prospect who will have shopped about 7 dealerships these days, who will be tough to close, and they'll earn a small paycheck if they sell it.

You got into this business because you saw the potential. It's there every day, but you won't get lucky and hit $100,000+ a year if you're just one of the crowd out there, hoping for a good 'up' today.

Here's another one of those choices you make every day. You're going to work tomorrow – that isn't a question or a choice. The only question, and your most important choice is...

"What will you do with tomorrow?
Will you develop your skills and use your time at work as effectively
as possible to build your business and guarantee your future –
or will you wait and hope you get lucky?"

Tip to remember...Luck is not a strategy!

Your Potential By Customer Type

We summarized 10 groups of prospects into those 5 categories we just covered based on their closing ratios. Looking at each group individually, how much potential do you see with each type?

Category/Type	Additional Unit Potential
1. Walk-Ins	____ extra units / mo.
2a. Incoming Sales Calls	____ extra units / mo.
2b. Internet Leads	____ extra units / mo.
3a. Referral Prospecting W/Prev. Cust	____ extra units / mo.
3b. Orphan Owners You Contact	____ extra units / mo.
3c. Outside Prospects You Bring In	____ extra units / mo.
3d. Service Prospects You Meet	____ extra units / mo.
3e. Your Friends & Acquaintances	____ extra units / mo.
4. Unsold Prospects	____ extra units / mo.
5. Repeat Customers Through Retention	____ extra units / mo.
Total Potential Above	_____ Additional Units Per Month
Your Average Commission Per Unit	$_____ Per Unit
Your Total Income Potential Above	$_____ **Per Mo.**
	$_____ **Per Yr...**

"8 units my first week after class!"

"Before Joe Verde training I was selling 6 to 8-cars. I went to my first Verde workshop late in the month and sold 8 cars in my first week back, and ended with 14 that month! Joe Verde training is different from any other training I've done in the past. It gives you the base knowledge in class and reinforcement back home with JVTN®." – Tim, Salesperson, Saskatchewan

CHAPTER 7

Why Talking Price To Select A Vehicle
Will Cost You Sales And Gross

I would never question that almost every prospect will want to talk about price, trade, down and payments before they're ready to take a vehicle home today. I also know you don't want to spend time with people you don't *think* can or will buy today because of the price.

But if you want to learn how to earn over $100,000, you're going to have to learn how to do the opposite and (bypass) price instead of trying to use price to help you select the right vehicle.

If you don't focus on price, you'll help them find the perfect vehicle, you'll build more value, they'll get more excited, and they'll step up and pay more, because it's the perfect vehicle (for them). That means you'll sell more cars, have more fun, make more money and send your customers home happier than ever before.

Why You Can't Talk Price

Price – Price – Price – Price – Price!

In class, we talk about how prospects jump online, go through the newspaper for pricing and to see what their trade is worth, grab a calculator and sit down to do their…

'Kitchen Table Budget' (KTB)

What's a 'Kitchen Table Budget'? The kitchen table is where 94% of the people sit down together to make their decisions about how much they think they can afford to pay for their new vehicle. They'll talk about the four areas that affect almost everyone when they're buying a vehicle: down payment, monthly payments, trade value and the price they'll pay.

85% of your prospects go through all of these numbers *before* they walk on the lot and tell you 'just looking'.

The catch is if you talk about any of these issues before you build enough value in the vehicle and before you get a commitment to own the vehicle, you'll lose sales almost every day you could have easily closed, and you'll lose gross profit on every vehicle you deliver.

We'll talk about their 'Kitchen Table Budgets' in the next chapter, but this brings up these common questions right away…

But why can't you talk price on the lot – prospects want to know how much it is before they look at a vehicle!

Besides, isn't finding out what they want to spend how you select the right vehicle?

My first five years, I would have argued with anybody who told me that I should present the vehicle first and then talk about price later. I would have said that by presenting first and talking about price later…

• *I might* spend an hour with someone and find out they were way over their head in payments and didn't have enough down payment to finance those 22" wheels, much less the car.

- Or *I might* end up spending an hour with someone and find out their credit was so bad they couldn't buy a candy bar with $1 down.

- Or *I might* spend an hour with someone and then find out they're so far upside down, they'd have to take a second on their house just to break even.

- Worse, if I spent the time to demo someone who can't buy or who can't afford to buy, *I might* miss a real deal while I'm with them.

I would have argued that it just didn't make sense to present first and talk price later. And I can even hear my first manager's words echoing in my head to reinforce the argument, "You better find out what they owe on their trade before you spend a lot of time with them, we have people all over the lot."

When I was with someone for more than a few minutes, he'd always ask me, "What's it gonna take to make a deal with them?" or "What payments are they looking for?"

Everything I was taught and all of my experience my first five years told me that pre-qualifying people before I went to the trouble to give them a presentation and demonstration made sense.

I honestly believed that finding out how much they had down, what they owed on their trade and what payments they were looking for was how you were supposed to select a vehicle for them to buy.

The key words in those arguments I made for talking price: I might!

If you'll re-read those bullet points, you'll find the word 'I might' in every reason I justified talking price. And it's true, you could spend time with people and they *might* not buy, for whatever reason.

The problem: What happens if you *don't* give everyone your best presentation and demonstration first, before you start talking price?

The words change from I might not sell them to I probably won't sell them – even if they came to buy – because they don't see the value in paying what it takes to purchase the vehicle.

How to deliver 50% more units right now!

If you're talking to an average number of prospects per month (60-75) and you're delivering 10 units – by spending the time with *everyone* to do your very best job, even though some won't buy and even though some can't buy, and even though you might miss another sale while you're with these people, you *will deliver 50% more vehicles than you're delivering now*.

> *The habit I had of focusing on price before*
> *I got my prospects excited about owning the vehicle*
> *was the costliest mistake I made my first five years.*

It's the costliest mistake you're probably making right now, too. I was just an 8-car guy those first five years, but even back then I knew I could have sold more cars if I'd consistently done the things I should have been doing – especially building more value.

I *could have done* a decent presentation if I wanted to, in fact I did when it sounded like I had a buyer. Because I put in so many hours, in real life, I *could have* sold 15 or 20 cars a month even with my weak selling skills and my crummy attitude. But I didn't because I took every shortcut I could and focused everything on price, which causes you to make two additional mistakes, that cost you sales:

Mistake #1:   Not giving everyone a demonstration.

Why?   Because 99% don't buy without a demonstration.

That means demonstrating a vehicle is a requirement to making a sale 99% of the time. If you pre-qualify based on the price, trade, down and payments they say they can afford, and then you decide they don't deserve a demo (or if you don't take control, assume the demo and make sure they get behind the wheel), you have guaranteed 'no sale', no matter how cheap you can sell the vehicle.

> *Only 30% to 40% actually get demos on a good day!*

Salespeople in our surveys and class freely admit they're only giving 30% to 40% of today's more informed prospects a demonstration. That means salespeople are only giving 3 or 4 people out of every 10 a great presentation and demonstration, hoping they'll buy anyway, and missing 3 sales for every one unit they deliver.

If you actually *think* you're giving 75% of your prospects a demonstration – there's a 99% chance you just aren't counting everybody. How about the service customer who said, "Don't waste time with me, they're just changing my oil," or the people who said, "We're in a hurry," the guy on his lunch hour who said, "Just looking," and the kid on the skateboard who said, "My Mom and Dad are getting me a car soon." Did you count all of them?

Have you ever sold a service customer, or that person in a hurry or anyone who said 'just looking' or got that kid to call Mom and Dad because he was so excited – and they bought today?

If you've been selling for more than a couple of months, the answers are yes, yes, yes and yes – and if you'll give more good demonstrations to everyone you meet, you'll keep selling more and more of the prospects most other salespeople won't even talk to.

Because of the 99% demo rule, when salespeople only let 3 or 4 out of 10 drive the vehicle – what do they guarantee?…Exactly, they've guaranteed 6 or 7 out of 10 *won't buy* – can't buy, didn't drive first. (If your goal is more sales, that isn't a logical choice.)

But watch those same salespeople spend hours selling price and trying to write people up who aren't sold on them, the product or the dealership. Then after a bad day, week, or month, watch them complain because the dealer doesn't bring in more traffic or because their manager doesn't work their deals right.

(Yes, I agree, again – we've all sold someone we didn't demo first. But if you count them all, it's less than 1% of the people you talk to, and those odds stink, so don't use this argument.)

Mistake #2:   **Talking price and not building value.**

Why?   You can't do both; talk price and build value.

There is no way to discuss price and build value at the same time, period, especially when you're dropping the price or negotiating.

If you want to close more sales and deliver a car today, every day, then you need to go back and review how the buying process works and get on JVTN® or come to class and learn how to handle price.

Has anyone ever paid you more than they said they would on the lot?

Have you ever talked price, trade, rates, down and payments on the lot and then sold someone a vehicle who ended up paying more than they said they would? Check the ones that are correct...

❑ Most people come up with *more down* than they said they would.

❑ Most people *take less for their trade* than they said they would.

❑ Most people *pay more for the vehicle* than they said they would.

❑ Most people make higher payments than they said they would.

Actually, wouldn't the better question be: Have you ever *not had* someone pay you more for the vehicle, not taken less for their trade, not come up with more down, or not made higher payments than they initially said they would?   ❑ Not very often.

From experience, I know 20% of you likely started *going off on the last question* with the common rant of, "You don't get it, our customers are different, and I had this guy yesterday, who only wanted our best price, blah, blah, blah..."

If that's you, if you aren't willing to count the real number of times someone *demands to get your best price first,* compared to the people who don't, you can't sell more. If you cling to a response you only get 5-10-20% of the time as your logic for doing it wrong 100% of the time – you should probably get a different job, because this one is never going to work out like you're hoping it will.

Back to what we were taught about price…

If you talk about price, down, payments and trades first, don't most of those turn into a back and forth (negotiation)?   ❑ Yes

Will that 'back and forth' price conversation (negotiation) on the lot make it easier or tougher for you to build rapport, easier or tougher to investigate, present, demonstrate and easier or tougher to build enough value to close the sale and deliver a vehicle today?

❑ It will be easier.

❑ Tougher, of course.

Put aside what we were taught and just use common sense...

If our goal is to make a sale and hold gross – when would be the best time to talk about *how high* a prospect's *payments* would be or *how much down* they'd need, or how *high your price is*, and *how little* they were really going to get for their trade...

❑ Before you get them excited about owning your vehicle?

❑ After they've found the perfect vehicle and are so excited they're ready to drive it off the lot right now, so they'll be more flexible on pricing and terms?

When you leave out the bad habits we've developed and what we've been taught in the past on this price conversation, both logic and common sense say that you need to stay off price, build value, get people excited, close the sale *and then talk about price.*

_____

"Before your sales workshop, I was at 8 units and $225 in commission. 90 days later, I'm averaging 12 units per month with $578 in commission per unit. I did what you said; I learned how to stay off price so I could build more value."
– Dave, Salesperson, Chrysler Dodge Jeep

_____

Note: I did the math for you on the comment (above) to show you the difference you could see in your paycheck if you start building value first. My math doesn't even count the other bonuses and spiffs Dave made for selling 50% more units each month.

Was   8 units x $225 per unit = $1,800 per month

Now   12 units x $578 per unit = $6,936 per month

Dave delivers 50% more units, and makes 4 times more money after he stopped talking about price, than he did when we was focusing on price to try to make the sale.

About You & Price

What % of the time do you really talk about price in each area?

1. On the phone on incoming sales calls ____ %
2. On Internet leads to get them in ____ %
3. On outgoing follow-up calls to get them back in ____ %
4. On the lot in my investigation (to select a vehicle) ____ %
5. When I'm presenting the vehicle ____ %
6. When I'm demonstrating the vehicle ____ %
7. When I'm trying to close the sale ____ %
8. When they have an objection ____ %
9. When I start the paperwork ____ %
10. Throughout the negotiation (instead of terms) ____ %

Total From Above (1,000% is maximum)... ____ %

Average % of the time that I spend
talking price when I try to sell. (Total ÷ 10)

If you see my mouth moving,
there's a ____ % chance I'm talking price.

"After selling for 19 years, I doubled my sales using JVTN®."

"After 19 years I was still only at 7 or 8 cars, but in the past year I've committed to training daily on JVTN®. I've learned to build value and stay off price, which has increased my gross 25%. In addition, I just sold 14 cars last month, doubling my previous average that I held for 19 years in the business! What a difference!" — *SK, Salesperson, Louisiana*

CHAPTER 8

Kitchen Table Budgets

How prospects decide what they want to pay.

Almost every family makes big budget decisions the same way, and in the same place – at the kitchen table.

When you understand the process, and how they come up with the range of figures in these four key areas, and then learn how and when to bring up price, trade value, down and payments, you'll consistently sell more units and hold more gross profit.

Kitchen Table Budgets

Let's look at how people decide to buy, how they determine their budget, and what *really happens* when you start talking about price *before* they're completely sold on *you, your dealership* and *the vehicle.*

To remind you…

- 78% of the people who walk on the lot buy
- 85% of the buyers *decided to buy before they left home*

When do Bob and Betty really start thinking about getting a new car?

We know the 'buying itch' usually starts around the 2-1/2 year mark. At this point, there's also a good chance they've been driving *not quite* the car they really wanted last time. Why isn't it the one they wanted? Because most prospects also get so bogged down in price, and focus so much on price they don't buy the right vehicle, so they trade more often and cost themselves a ton in the long run.

And they're very likely to do the exact same thing again, unless you avoid price and focus on value, so you can help them find the perfect vehicle and fit the perfect vehicle into their budget this time.

Once they get the itch, they start mentally picturing that perfect vehicle. Then they start to notice everything they dislike about the car they're driving now. About this same time, every time they look around, they see one of the vehicles on their 'perfect vehicle' list.

Next, it's time to justify why they need to trade NOW!

After a few weeks of seeing the perfect vehicle everywhere, they start justifying why they need to trade. And very soon Bob and Betty start checking out cars online or in the paper.

They learn more about the vehicle and the pricing. They also start checking the 'for sale by owner' ads online and in the paper to see what a vehicle like theirs is selling for. Then they figure theirs must be much nicer and should be worth a thousand or two more.

Then come the dealer price ads online and in the paper. They see the low ball ads on the stripped down model. Sure, they did this last time, too, and understand it's probably the low-end model, but hope they might be able to wrangle that same deal on a loaded one with 22" wheels and the rear entertainment system for the kids.

Next they start talking about trading and then the itch turns into urgency; "Honey, I think we need to get a new car this weekend before we start having real problems with ours."

Everyone loves getting new cars, so when their 'honey' says, "OK, but we need to make sure we can afford it," that's when the conversation moves to the kitchen table and to the four areas that affect their budget: price, trade, down and payments.

Kitchen Table Budgets (KTB)

- **On Payments:** They're paying $375 now because they put a little extra down last time. But they saw some prices in the paper for as low as $399 on the model they want (they avoided the fine print). But what the heck, why not try for that payment? If it doesn't work, they figure they could spend $450, and if they had to, they could do $475. And if it really got down to it and they watered down the kid's milk to save money, they could do $500, but that's about it.

- **On Down Payments:** They saw ads for zero down financing so they figure they'll try that, too. And if it doesn't work, they could put $500 down with no problem. If they needed to, they could come up with another $500 – and if they found a car they really liked, they'd be willing to hit the secret stash and put $1,500 down.

- **On Their Trade:** They saw one on the Internet like theirs for $9,000 but Bob figured theirs is much nicer so they're hoping to get $10,500, but they'd take $9,000 if they had to. Then Bob looked up his car online and he couldn't believe wholesale was only $7,800 – so they agreed they'd take that if they had to. And if it really got down to it, they want to trade so badly, they'd take $7,642.55, because that's their payoff until the end of the month.

- **On Price:** On your manufacturer's site, the fully loaded one they want retails for $34,896. But they saw a local ad in the paper on one for $26,999. Sure, they know it's an ad car, but they'll plead insanity on pricing. They'd go $30,000 if they had to, and maybe $32,000 but they don't want to spend much more than that.

So do you have a deal at their 'hope to' figures in those four areas? No way – not even close and _even they know it_. Will they pay more? Of course, they always do – _they already plan to pay more_ than their 'hope to' numbers and they've _already factored that into their budget_.

The average salesperson wants to talk about the money _quick,_ so they can select the right (priced) vehicle. But when you ask Bob and Betty what they want to spend, will you get the highest numbers from their KTB, or their lowest? _Absolutely, you're guaranteed to get the lowest figures they can possibly hope to pay._

Salespeople lock-up most deals at impossible figures...

Why? Because once Bob or Betty say those 'hope to' figures out loud, they'll have to defend those numbers throughout the sale, _even though they're willing to pay thousands more for the vehicle._

Here's A Quick Recap Of Their Kitchen Table Budget

Highlight how much this prospect is _willing to pay_ for the vehicle, how much they've _already agreed they could put down,_ what they've _agreed they could afford_ in payments, and the _lowest they've agreed they'd take for their trade._

Trade	Price
$ 7,642.^{55}	$34,896 MSRP
$ 7,800	$32,000
$ 9,000	$30,000
$10,500	$26,999

Down	Payments
$1,500	$ 500
$1,000	$ 475
$ 500	$ 450
$ 0	$ 399

Even though they've already agreed to pay more, here's how the conversation will usually go with 'Bob and Betty Buyer' and a typical salesperson who talks price on every deal.

Salesperson: Hi – how can I help you?

Prospect: We're just looking. (Reflex objection)

Salesperson: Do you know what you want to look at?

Prospect: Yeah, we want a blue x40, loaded with 22" wheels and a rear entertainment system. Do you have one?

Salesperson: Sure, we have one right over here. What kind of payments were you guys looking for?

Prospect: We don't want to go over $399 – that's what we can buy it for at ZZ Motors, we saw an ad this weekend.

Salesperson: Wow – that's low, how much were you putting down?

Prospect: We saw an ad with no money down, and don't want to put any money down, either.

Salesperson: Well, I hope your trade is worth a lot, what do you want for it?

Prospect: We want $11,000 for it. (They just got cocky.) And we saw an x40 exactly like this advertised for $26,999.

Salesperson: You really can't buy this loaded x40 for that price, and with nothing down your payments will be closer to $800, why don't we look at a less expensive model?

Prospect: (Push back time) No, we don't want a different one, we know what we want and that's all we'll pay. If you guys can't do that, then we'll just go somewhere else.

Salesperson: Hold on Bob, can you help me just a little bit on the price? We'll make you a good deal, but you're looking at a stripped down ad vehicle in the paper, not one fully loaded like this. You gotta help me out some.

Prospect: (More push back) Nope, that's it – that's all we'll do. Come on Betty, let's go.

Salesperson: Hey now, hold on a minute … if we could do what you're looking for, are you ready to take it home now?

Prospect: If you can do it, we'll take it – but that's it, that's all we're going to pay.

Salesperson: Do you need to drive it first?

Prospect: No, just see if you can do this.

Salesperson: OK, let me go check with my manager real quick.

Salesperson: Boss, I've got a tough one here. I have some people who want the blue x40 for $26,999, they don't want to put any money down, they want a $399 payment and $11,000 for their trade. Can we do it for that?

Manager:	Will they buy it today?
Salesperson:	They said they would.
Manager:	Do you have a write-up?
Salesperson:	They wouldn't come inside, they just want to know if we can do the deal at their figures.
Manager:	Did they drive it?
Salesperson:	Nah, they wouldn't drive it – I think they drove one somewhere else, they just want to know if we can do it.
Manager:	All right – get me the keys to their trade, *and next time don't bring me any more deals until people have driven the car.* #%##% I've told you that before and I'm not kidding this time, this better be the last time you bring me a deal like this!
Salesperson:	OK, sure Boss, it won't happen again.
Manager:	What's their name?
Salesperson:	I don't know, they didn't say.

Can we be serious for a minute? If you recognize any part of this dialogue, do you really think the next time you take a deal like this to the desk, it will end up any different than it did the last time you brought one in?

Go back and read about 'The Buying & Selling Process,' in chapter 4, because these first 2 or 3 minutes you're with the prospect are critical. In that time, you have to start warming them up, getting control with questions and *you have to avoid talking about price* or you'll end up at their lowest figures in these Kitchen Table Budgets.

In this example, it started with the wrong greeting and there was no control at all of the selling process. When you lack control, that sets you up for questions from your prospects about price, which leads to you getting off track and completely away from building value in owning the vehicle.

But if you do this *right* from the beginning, you can almost completely eliminate the opportunity for the prospect to even bring up their Kitchen Table Budget numbers – and you'll get control of the sale right away.

So what does 'do it right' mean?

Again, we spend 16 hours in class teaching you how to warm them up, bypass price, build value and close the sale – and there are a few hundred chapters on JVTN® about selling and dealing with price, so there's no way to teach you the entire process in this book.

In class and on JVTN® we show you how to move any price talk out of the conversation when it comes up on the lot, when you're closing and when you're negotiating. And we'll show you how to turn price objections into 'budget concerns' so that you can focus on terms in your negotiation, instead of price. That's critical, since 94% of the people make payments instead of paying cash.

Even if you haven't been to class yet, you can still make changes in how you sell starting tomorrow that will improve your sales and income. Just finish this book, and then read it again slowly two or three times, and you'll increase your sales and income right away.

"From 8 to 14 the month after class."

"Joe, I recently attended your Sales Workshop and I can't even tell you how great I'm doing. Before class, I averaged 8 a month thinking I was doing as much as I can. One month after class I jumped to 14 units because I continued to train on JVTN® and began to really understand the Basics and what it means to be in sales. I've heard you say, 'Common sense is just not that common,' and couldn't agree more. Sometimes we need a refresher of what it means to be in sales and your training does that and more! Thanks." – Greg, Salesperson, Texas

Kitchen Table Budgets

These are the three biggest mistakes I make when talking to customers about pricing and their budget that cost me sales.

1. _____

   Why? _____

   _____

   To eliminate this mistake, I will... _____

   _____

2. _____

   Why? _____

   _____

   To eliminate this mistake, I will... _____

   _____

3. _____

   Why? _____

   _____

   To eliminate this mistake, I will... _____

   _____

"8 cars in 10 days and upped my gross $1,750 per unit!"

"Before attending your Closing & Negotiation workshop I was averaging 12 cars per month, with $650 gross per unit.

After class I started utilizing JVTN® and presenting the deal with confidence and followed the steps and scripts exactly how I was taught in class and online. I sold 8 cars in 10 days with an average gross of $2,400!

I was at the bottom in gross and units, and now I'm at the top. Thank you, Joe!" — *Kevin, Salesperson, RI*

CHAPTER 9

Your Secrets To Success

Drum roll, please...

To get to $100,000+ you have to meet 'SHAC'

If I were to add up everything I've learned about selling
and growth, there are hundreds of things you need to
learn and do. However, almost everything falls into just
these four categories!

S H A C

I went from 8 to 38 units because I learned these four
secrets and that means you can, too. These are the *only*
four areas you need to focus on and master, to grow
and improve year after year.

SHAC

SKILLS

Your *skill level* in sales completely controls your success. To earn over $100,000, there are hundreds of skills you can develop. But don't let 'hundreds' scare you, because there are a few quick skills you can learn in class and on JVTN® within just 90 days so you can earn two or three times what the average salesperson earns.

The good news about skill development and growth: You'll never run out of new skills to develop or out of old skills that need to be improved. Either way, if you develop a new skill, or improve an old one, you'll sell more units, have more fun and make more money.

A Few Skills For Starters: Greeting, Investigating, Building Rapport, Presenting, Demonstrating the Vehicle, Demonstrating the Features (Navigation, iDrive, etc.), Using Evidence Manuals, Closing, Overcoming Objections, Bypassing Price, Setting Up the Negotiation, Write-Ups, Negotiating, Paperwork, Introduction to Finance, Turning Properly, Delivery, Follow-Up, Prospecting, Controlling the Sale, Asking Questions, Listening, Communication, Organization, Time Management, Tracking, Goal Setting, Planning, Incoming Calls, Outgoing Calls, Internet Leads, Appointments, Getting Appointments to Show, Writing Skills for Emails and Mail-Outs, and hundreds of related minor skills.

Step 1: Highlight the skills above you know you need to work on and then develop your plan to improve.

The 3 most important areas you want to develop first to close more sales and sell a car every day are...

 • The New Basics™ – The Steps of Selling
 • Effective Questioning Skills
 • Effective Closing and Objection Handling Skills

Mastering these three skill <u>sets</u> will take you to 20 or 30 units per month, if you go to work to work and apply what you learn.

sHac

HABITS

Habits are *as critical*, or maybe even more critical than Skills.

Why? Because you can have great Presentation and Closing Skills, but if you have the habit of Pre-Qualifying Prospects, by default, you also have the habit of *not* giving everyone a great Presentation and Demonstration, which by default means you *can't* Close more sales because 99% of the people *won't buy* without a Demonstration.

No demo means no sale!

It's the same with Follow-Up. Your sold customers and the people you didn't sell today may really like you, but if you don't develop your Follow-Up Skills, and if you don't develop the Habit of doing your Follow-Up daily, it's another absolute fact that by default, you'll be sending most of your prospects to your competition down the street.

A Few Critical Habits...

Following The New Basics™ 100% of the time with 100% of the prospects, following the Closing and Objections process, Staying off Price on the Lot and on the Phone, setting up your Negotiation properly, completing your Finance and Delivery Paperwork correctly, doing Unsold Follow-Up daily, reviewing Your Daily Dozen checklist (a dozen good habits), Getting Organized, Evaluating every Sale or missed Sale, Going to Work to Work and the habit of Learning More Every Day!

With good skills and good habits, you'll definitely
close more deals and deliver more units!

s h **A** c

ATTITUDE

"Act enthusiastic and you'll be enthusiastic!" – *Dale Carnegie*

Attitude isn't just about smiling and being happy. Sure, that's important, but your Attitude about selling cars, your dealership, your product, your managers, developing Skills and Habits, and even your Attitude about your next prospect determines your success.

No matter how successful you want to be, your Skills and Work Habits will make or break you. *But of Skills, Habits and Attitude, your Attitude is most important.*

Why? Think about it. Doesn't your Attitude control everything you do? If you don't like selling, you won't work on your Skills or your Habits. The same is true if you don't like your dealership, your managers, selling cars or talking to people – you won't work on getting better and you'll never do your best to sell a vehicle!

We talked about how important Follow-Up is, but doesn't your Attitude about Follow-Up determine whether you develop that Skill, and whether you actually do your Follow-Up every day?

Absolutely! Until you enthusiastically buy into the benefits of Follow-Up, you won't be developing related Skills or Habits. And that means you'll miss the easiest sales you could be making.

The same is true with giving everyone a Great Presentation and Demonstration. You may have Great Skills and Habits, but when you first meet that prospect, your Attitude about them determines just how *great* your Presentation will be, if they get one at all. Pre-Qualifying is a Habit that kills your sales right now and is one of the hardest habits to break, because it's tied to your Attitude about whether your prospects look, act and sound like buyers.

The most important Attitude you need to develop is about 'YOU'!

Before you can grow and improve, you have to *sell yourself* on becoming a professional in sales. Once you make this important decision – that's when the fun really begins in sales!

s h a C

CHOICE OF CUSTOMERS

Does it matter to you how much you make each month, or is selling just a hobby? I hope you said you want to make money. If you do want to make more money, would it make sense to focus on the easiest people to close who pay you the most, or the toughest prospects your dealership can supply who pay the least?

Which prospect doesn't usually shop price, is 6 times easier to close, pays you 40% more, gives you great CSI and will buy more vehicles in the future from you, if you do your Follow-Up?

   ❏ A Fresh Walk-In Prospect   ❏ A Repeat Customer

A guy on a plane asked me, "How come there aren't any pros who sell cars?" I reminded him there are tons of pros in our business, *but you don't find most of them standing out front waiting for an 'up'.* The real pros are too busy working with their own customers.

My salesperson at the local Mercedes dealership was # 1 in the store, the store was in the top 5 in the nation and he didn't take any walk-in traffic. Another salesperson, Clark, who attends our workshops made over $400,000 selling used cars in a town of 15,000 people, and he doesn't take walk-in traffic, either.

Again, you can be an aggressive go-getter, develop your skills, become a Lean, Mean, Closing Machine and earn $100,000 plus each year by putting in a ton of hours. But I don't know more than a handful of high achievers in our business who don't have a solid base of customers they can count on who will buy again and again and who will refer all of their family and friends to them, too.

The best part about developing your customer base is that...

   • You can control your own income in sales.

   • You control your hours worked (work smart, not long).

This fourth secret is *the gift that keeps on giving* and *guarantees your continued success in sales* for the rest of your career.

YOU & SHAC

Skills   3 Most Important Skills I Need To Work On Now:

- _____
- _____
- _____

Habits   3 Most Important Habits I Need To Work On Now:

- _____
- _____
- _____

Attitudes   3 Most Important Attitude Adjustments I Need:

- _____
- _____
- _____

Choice of Customers

My Current Sales & Income Per Month By Customer Type

% of sales & income from prospects my dealership supplies me with...

Walk-In __ % $ ____   Phone __ % $ ____ Internet __ % $ ____

% of sales & income from prospects I generate on my own...

Repeat __ % $ ____ Referral __ % $ ____ Be-Backs __% $ ____

My own Outside Prospects I bring into the dealership   __ % $ ____

Dealership Customers (Service / Parts) I bring up front   __ % $ ____

If you don't know the answers – that's the point:

Track everything – especially your sales by customer type!

CHAPTER 10

The Traps Most Salespeople Fall Into

We've covered a lot of different ways you can reach $100,000 plus. Most salespeople will never hit those levels though, because they fall into the common traps that keep them stuck in the 8-car rut their entire career.

One common element in these traps is hanging around with the average and below average salespeople. So if you're serious about becoming a pro, as nice as they may be, an average salesperson can't help you get any further in sales than they are now. In fact, it is practically guaranteed they'll hold you back.

Here's a great tip...

Only take advice from people
who are as successful as you want to be.

The Traps Most Salespeople Fall Into

This is really simple: If you start selling cars, or if you already sell cars and want to improve, don't get caught in these traps.

If you do fall into these traps, odds are you'll land a career in the huddle as an average or below average salesperson. Chances are you'll also jump dealership to dealership hoping that will solve your problems, or you'll just quit and get out of the car business.

Avoid these traps and you'll sell cars, have fun, make money and enjoy a great career in sales.

The Biggest Mistakes Salespeople Make

1. They want to "fit in" so bad, most salespeople, especially new salespeople, can't stay away from the huddle.

Every new person who goes to work anywhere wants to *fit in* with the group. That's natural, and to a point it makes perfectly good sense to want to be part of a team. Just make sure you pick the *right* team, because the wrong team will destroy your career.

My first five years, not only did I head straight to the huddle the first day I was hired; I was drawn to the huddle like a magnet, anytime I didn't have anything to do. Besides, what better way to make myself feel good about not selling more cars than to find someone else to invite to my 'pity party' and to give me some new excuses, if I didn't have enough of my own?

Solution: Walk away from the huddle and never look back.

Write this on some business cards; put one in your pocket, one on your phone, plus put copies anywhere else you can see this question:

"Am I doing the most productive thing possible right now?"

When you read it, if you aren't, then go do something that will help you sell a vehicle now or in the future.

2. They never develop their core skills in sales, and they stop even attempting to learn more after just a few weeks.

We'll cover a list of skills you need to develop in a later chapter, but if you were trying to condense all that you need to know into just a few short sound bites, you have to learn how to...

- Get people on the lot
- Sell them while they're there
- Keep them forever as loyal customers

The huddle can't help you develop these skills, so you need to take this upon yourself. You have to learn how to *generate your own floor traffic*, learn how to *sell and negotiate* so you can deliver 30% to 40% of the people you talk to, and you have to learn how to *retain* your customers to grow every year.

There are hundreds of major and minor skills you need in sales, which means even after you develop your *core* skills, you need a *consistent* continuing education program to keep developing new skills, and retraining on the skills you have.

3. Most salespeople quickly learn how to justify staying average!

For most people, getting into 'commission only' sales is tough enough, especially with no real training. Add a few failed attempts at making a sale and before long, pride and ego step in to help justify why it isn't our fault that we aren't selling more.

Solution: Stop explaining to everyone why you aren't selling more and use that time to develop your skills, so you can sell more cars.

Review the upcoming skills chapter and check the reasons why you aren't selling more units and making more money. I can tell you now, even the 'best of the best' salespeople can check off a dozen plus skills on any given day that they need to improve.

Don't get bogged down on how many skills you need, and just start attacking them, one at a time. What you'll also find is that many of the things you need to improve aren't just the skills you need to develop. Remember – huddles, your work habits, attitudes, enthusiasm, confidence, and much more – also matter.

4. They quickly learn how to pre-qualify their customers.

78% of the people who walk on your lot will be buying a vehicle, 85% of them specifically came to buy and 90% will buy within a week of stopping at the first dealership, with you or without you.

Tip: You can't guess who those 78% are, and you can prove it.

Remember your first few days on the lot? You didn't know anything about anything. You didn't know about the stats, you just *assumed* (correctly) that everybody who came on the lot was there to buy, so you did your best and you sold a few cars.

Even when they asked you, "What's my trade worth?" back then you were new and said, "I don't know," and you got back to showing them cars *with enthusiasm*. Same thing when they asked you about discounts on price, trade, rebates, interest rates or how much down they'd need or how much the payments would be. You just kept repeating your logical script..."I don't know."

Then with help from the huddle, you got the 6-week on the job course on how to end up just 'average' in sales...

How long did it really take for you to become an expert – a few tips from the 6-car guy, and then talking to maybe 100 prospects? In just a few short weeks, almost all new salespeople go from enthusiastically giving everyone a great presentation and demonstration and selling some vehicles to explaining why it isn't their fault their sales drop off. And their Support Group always helps them by blaming the market, the economy, their dealer, etc. Soon, they even start to blame their customers.

We track and chart every salesperson's performance at our Dealer / Manager Workshops. Their homework the first night after class is to chart and graph every one of their salespeople's unit sales for the last 12 months.

Almost every new salesperson's chart says exactly the same thing. They knew nothing and sold some vehicles in the beginning, then they had a better month their 2nd month. By their 3rd or 4th month though, their sales drop back to where they started or lower.

Is it their fault? Maybe not, if they didn't get the right *initial training* and education when they were hired. Let's not kid each other, only getting that average of 7.4 hours of training to sell to today's buyers, just won't cut it.

On JVTN®, our Fast Start training outline for all salespeople (new and experienced) takes most people 60 to 90 days to complete *correctly*, sometimes longer. They start learning on day one, get their core skills down the next 90 days and then train 5 days a week on JVTN® for the rest of their career to start improving all of their initial skills – and developing more.

Step 1: Stop pre-qualifying your prospects right now.

You don't need to know what your prospects want to spend, you just need to know *what they want and why they want it,* so you can get them excited enough about the vehicle to spend whatever it takes.

Step 2: Step away from those guys in the huddle – they'll ruin your career before it starts. Instead, get to class and on JVTN® for a real education in sales. Even while you're learning and still developing your skills, start giving everyone great presentations again and you'll double your sales and triple your income.

5. **Average salespeople spend their careers standing out front just waiting for a walk-in customer, instead of building their business**.

Why is this a trap? That's easy...

- Walk-in prospects close at 8-12% per 100.
- Repeat customers close at 70-80% per 100.
- Most walk-in prospects are tough to deal with.
- Repeat customers are a pleasure to deal with.
- Most walk-in prospects are the price shoppers.
- Repeat customers come back in because they like you.
- Walk-in prospects pay less in gross profit than anyone.
- Repeat customers pay at least 40% more in gross profit.

The 'walk-in' prospects most salespeople spend their lives in this business waiting for are the least productive, most price-focused, hardest to close prospects you will ever talk to in sales.

Solution: Stop waiting for an 'up' and generate your own traffic.

How to sell 8 to 10 more cars this month: Make just 5 calls every day to people you've sold, call 5 service customers from last week, make 5 easy prospecting calls to people you know, and wander out to service and talk to just 5 people a day.

That's 20 contacts per day, 100 per week and that means every month you'll talk to 400 *more* people than you normally do. That's 5 or 6 times as many contacts as you're making each month right now, and that means more sales. No matter how good or bad you are in sales, if you talk to another 400 people, you'll bump into buyers and you'll sell another 8 or 10 units, period.

And how long will those fifteen 5-minute phone calls or 5-minute contacts in service really take?

Exactly, about 90 minutes – or less time than most salespeople spend in the huddle each day talking about how slow it is.

6. **Most salespeople put in a lot of hours and most have good intentions, but they lack clear goals and a plan to succeed!**

There's a huge difference between having great intentions, working hard, and spending a ton of time in the dealership trying to sell something – compared to having clear goals, a definite daily work plan, and focusing on *selling activities* all day.

The problem isn't with a salesperson's *intent* when they work long and hard. Of course their intention is to sell more and make more money. But good intentions aren't goals. And working hard isn't a plan. And doing unproductive things all day won't equal sales. (See "Setting Goals To Double Sales" on JVTN®.)

Now go back through these 6 again, and highlight the traps you're stuck in right now – then get out of them quick!

Peer pressure is one of your toughest challenges...

Other than these traps, one of the toughest challenges you'll face on your road to more success will be the peer pressure from your own group of friends in the dealership. Unless they're on the same track you're on, reading this book and attending our classes with you, once they realize you've gotten serious and are there for just one reason: to sell more cars, have more fun and make more money, be prepared for the backlash from those *friends.*

When I started selling cars again, almost everyone at the dealership was a friend, or at least I thought they were. As the pinstriper, I knew everybody pretty well. We went camping, fishing, boating and to ball games together. But as soon as they saw I was serious about selling and since I never signed up for the huddle, they started the negative stuff gradually, but the gloves came off pretty quick.

Here again, this is where that book "Choices" came in handy. I had to remember the choices I was faced with – keeping my friends in the huddle happy by hanging around with them, not being very successful and wasting my days like they were doing – or – going to work to work and using my skills to do everything I could to sell more cars and make more money and risk losing those friends.

I made my decision. I decided I was going to work to make a living, not friends. Now none of us sit by those campfires together anymore.

My goal in our classes, on JVTN® and in this book is to help you with everything I know you'll face on your way to closing more sales and selling a car today, every day. I want to save you some time, save you some of that long, hard work and show you how to take shortcuts to develop your skills faster, so you can take the only true shortcut to success – personal improvement.

I want to show you how to work smart by learning to set clear goals and writing a plan to succeed, instead of living on the 'I hope it all works out' plan. I want to give you the information on selling skills you need to develop and show you how to earn professional wages.

Like my friends at work, most of your peers aren't going to support you – so do what's best for you and your family and don't look back.

**So that you don't spend a career just working hard,
set clear activity goals so that you're productive every day.**

Leave out the highballs and fill in 5 sales *activity* goals today that you'll commit to achieving in the next 30 days, and then break those into weekly and daily goals.

Don't write down your 'hope to' or 'I'll try to' numbers. Write in your 'will do' numbers, and then don't go home each day until you've completed these activities.

1. How many total unsold follow-up, prospecting and retention calls will you make in the *next 30 days?* ____

    The math: How many calls is that *per day?* ____

2. How many service customers will you talk to this *month?* ____

    The math: How many will that be *each day?* ____

3. How many prospects will you personally bring into the dealership *this month?* ____

    The math: How many will that be each *week?* ____

4. How many *out of 10* will you demo this month? ____

5. Remembering the average sale is closed after the 5th closing attempt, how many times will you attempt to close every sale this month? ____

*Fill in the blanks above, reach those daily
activity goals and you'll sell more units every month.*

\-\-\-\-\-\-\-\-\-\-\-\-\-\-\-

"I went from 6 to 16."

"Joe, before your class I averaged 6 units per month and I was struggling to even do that. In class I learned the importance of investigation and finding my customer's wants and needs.

Now, instead of just finding them a car, I help them find their 'perfect' car and price isn't an objection. I also started tracking my activities and setting monthly goals in your planners. By doing both of these things, I sold 16 units my first month back!" Paola, Sales, Ford, Kentucky

CHAPTER 11

The Skills You Need In Sales

Too many people in sales, and even managers think that 'selling' is either something you're born with that you can do naturally, or that you can't learn to sell at all.

That just isn't true!

There are definitely a lot of 'natural talents' that will help you sell, but nothing can replace saying *exactly* the right words at *exactly* the right time.

Whether you're new, or just want to sell even more, read this section carefully and check off the skills you need to work on to move up to your next level in sales and to hit that $100,000 plus range in income.

The Skills You
Need To Sell A Car Today

We've talked about getting you ready to sell more and earn more by better understanding your market, your customers and prospects and your real potential in sales.

We also discussed your secrets to success in sales, explained the buying and selling processes so you have a clearer picture of what you have to accomplish, analyzed the budget decision-making process (KTB) your customers go through to buy expensive products, and covered how price talk on the lot will make it tougher for you to build the value you need to make the sale.

Now it's time to cover the skills you need to sell a vehicle today, tomorrow, and to build your business for the future.

In general, to hit over $100,000 a year, you have to...

- Know your *product* inside out and know your competitor's products, too.

- Ask the right *questions* at the right time to... control the conversation and the selling process, build rapport, investigate, build value, close, overcome and close on objections on the lot, get referrals, get names when people don't buy, make appointments, prospect, follow-up, close and overcome objections in the negotiation process – and negotiate a win/win every time at maximum gross profit and with perfect CSI.

- Bypass or rephrase *price* questions on phone and Internet leads.

- Build your own floor traffic through follow-up, prospecting and turning incoming calls and leads into appointments that show.

- Know and follow The New Basics™ of Selling, including how to close, overcome objections, set up the negotiation, and the 3-Pass negotiation process.

*Another secret to making over $100,000 is to develop
the skills most salespeople never even think about.*

Why Do You Need Continuing Education?

> *I asked my dentist why I needed to
> floss my teeth every day and he said...*
>
> *"You don't really need to. Only floss
> the teeth <u>every day</u>, that you want to keep!"*

You train every day for the same reason; so you can develop and then hold onto the skills you've developed.

How to get more out of this book...

Like I said early on; if you want to remember what you've read that will help you improve, you'll have to slow down. Take notes, list exactly what you want to work on, write clear goals on when and how you'll develop those skills, and then practice, drill and rehearse something every day, not just one time.

You should already have a huge list in your 3-ring binder on improvements you want to make in the SHAC categories, and you'll definitely fill your binder by the time you finish this chapter.

Improvement takes planning...

- What have you learned that you need to improve?
- How will you use what you've learned?
- Which Skill, Habit, Attitude or Customer-type (S, H, A, C) will you work on first?
- What do you want to accomplish with that S, H, A, or C?
- When will you start working on each item on your list?

Tip: Read this book again right away. Highlight key points and take extra notes on everything you want to remember and improve.

Repetition: We all learn through the repetition of seeing, hearing, and doing. The more often you read this, and the more often you practice what you're learning, the more you'll remember.

*If you read a book, or go through a JVTN® chapter 6 times,
and then practice, drill and rehearse each time, you'll remember and
be able to use 50% of what you've read and practiced!*

A Checklist Of Skills You Need
To Move To Your Next Level In Sales

No matter what level you're at in sales today, you can always move up another notch to sell more units, hold more gross profit, get better CSI, build your customer base and improve your income.

We've talked about your potential, your customers and what it takes to make more sales today. Now it's time to *evaluate* your current skill level in as many different areas as possible, so you'll be able to identify exactly what you want to improve.

Because there are so many skills you need in sales, you'll find some skills may slip here and there, even 'solid' skills you've worked on real hard. That means you'll want to go through this *evaluation* list every month, or at least every 90 days so you can maintain and improve.

You also need to track everything you do, so you can set clear goals for improvement in areas there, too. With your tracking and your evaluations, you'll be able to *target the exact training on JVTN®* you need to improve in those areas.

Because different people reading this are in so many different levels in sales, I've broken these checklists into 3 groups…

1. Moving from below 10 units per month *up to* 10 or 12

2. Getting from 10 or 12 *up to* 15 to 20 units each month

3. Moving from 20 to 30+ units to wherever you want to be

This isn't an exact science, because there are so many variables that affect your sales production. That's why you need to track what you do and then realistically, and honestly evaluate your skills.

Follow these guidelines, and you'll find that growth is easy, and just a natural event as you develop these skills. Pick a couple of the things you aren't doing now, and start getting better today.

Don't get overwhelmed with these lists. None of us is ever at the top of our game in every skill, every day. That's why you train and practice daily.

How To Improve To Your Next Level

No matter what level you're at today in sales...

If you're stuck at under 10 units per month, or stuck at 40, the first thing you have to figure out is *why* you've settled there.

And let me be clear, this is not a checklist of negatives to point out how bad you are in sales, even if you check everything. This is a list of the skills, work habits, attitudes, customer choices, and other choices and processes that when you improve, you'll grow.

Tip: Read through or thumb through these next few pages quickly. Then come back here and start over – and check every question or statement that (honestly) applies to you so you'll know exactly what to work on to improve and grow.

Let's Start With You, Personally…

❑ I'm not really sold on being in sales

❑ I seem to lack the motivation to try harder

❑ I'm a little, or somewhat uncomfortable on 'commission only'

❑ I'm not very organized, and waste too much of my day

❑ I'm fairly well-organized, but still waste too much of my day

❑ I don't really come to work to work, I could easily do more

❑ I'm easily distracted at work by other people or things

❑ I've gotten trapped in the huddle

❑ I'm easily influenced by the other salespeople

❑ I'm easily intimidated by the other salespeople

❑ I'm sometimes or often intimidated by some of my prospects

❑ I dress the way I did in my last job, not like the pro you describe

❑ I have low financial needs, and don't need to make much money

❑ I lack confidence in myself as a salesperson

❑ I have low expectations of myself in sales

❑ I do not have clear goals on what I want to accomplish in sales

About Selling…

❑ I sorta do, but I don't really understand 'sales'

❑ I'm uncomfortable trying to 'sell' people things

❑ I haven't had much training on how to sell

❑ I'm not very comfortable around a lot of my customers

❑ I sometimes feel awkward and unsure of what to say

❑ I spend most of my day waiting for a prospect

❑ I pre-qualify my prospects on price to *select* a vehicle

❑ I pre-qualify almost everyone to determine if they *can* buy

❑ I don't treat everyone as a buyer *today*

❑ I don't do the best job I'm capable of with each prospect

❑ I don't really listen very well when I'm with a prospect

❑ I have a hard time staying focused when I'm with a prospect

❑ I spend a lot of time talking price, trade, down or payments

❑ I need to improve my appearance to make a better 1ˢᵗ Impression

❑ I greet people with some version of "Can I help you?"

❑ I don't spend much time, or enough time, building rapport

❑ I don't spend much time, or enough time, investigating

❑ I give fewer than 75% of my prospects a good presentation

❑ I don't know enough *specific* product knowledge to cover FABs

❑ I spend too much time just *telling* people things

❑ I give fewer than 75% of my prospects a good demonstration

❑ I don't control the sale very well

❑ I don't ask many, or enough questions to find their hot buttons

❑ I don't introduce my prospects to service

❑ I don't have an evidence manual, or don't use it if I have one

❑ I usually focus on price in most of my closing questions

❑ I use the worst type of closing questions (yes or no)

❑ I'm fearful of trying to close because I may hear "No" and I don't know what to do next

❑ I don't ask for the order at least 5 times with each prospect

❑ I don't really know what to do when I get objections

❑ I focus on price, trade, down or payments when I get objections

❑ I don't try to write-up people I don't think *can* or *will* buy

❑ I write a lot of people up who are loosely committed, if at all

❑ I don't follow procedures and I take shortcuts in the write-up process

❑ I usually work my managers harder than I work my prospects

❑ I'm not very comfortable in the negotiation

❑ I'm afraid I'll lose the sale if I try to take control in the negotiation

❑ I'm not very good in the negotiation

❑ When I sell a vehicle, there are a lot of loose ends in my paperwork

❑ Other than my CSI call or letter, I don't follow-up after the sale

❑ If I don't sell the vehicle, I don't get their contact information

❑ If I don't sell the vehicle, I don't follow-up to get them back in

❑ I don't have a follow-up *process* in place for my unsold prospects

❑ I don't get someone else, a manager or another salesperson, involved when I can't close the sale today

❑ When I do get someone else involved, I usually wait until it's too late for anybody to save it

A few more things about selling and building your business.

❑ I don't have a follow-up *process* in place for my *sold* customers

❑ I *don't follow-up* my sold prospects to generate future business

❑ I don't handle *incoming sales calls* correctly to get 90% appointments

❑ I either talk *price* or try to *educate* prospects on the phone

❑ I do not have a 'show' ratio of 60% on my phone appointments

❑ I don't track all of my selling opportunities; floor traffic by type of prospect, incoming sales calls, Internet leads, etc.

❑ I don't track all of my selling activities; presentations, demonstrations, write-ups, outgoing prospecting calls, etc.

❑ I don't track all of my sales by type, type of prospect, total income

❑ I don't track my unit sales by my most recent 90 day average

❑ I do not chart and graph my units and income month to month

❑ I don't use my 90 day (current average) to set improvement goals

❑ I don't have clear, written, specific goals for the next 12 months

❑ I don't use the VSA®, or a planner or daily organizer to make sure I stay focused and on track at work each day

❑ I don't have a Master List I use to follow-up and prospect

❑ I don't contact my previous customers every 90 days by phone and every 45 days by mail

❑ I don't send my newsletter to all of my prospects every 45 days

❑ I don't know the simple 5 question referral script

❑ I don't make 5 calls per day to follow-up my sold customers and I don't use the referral script on each call

❑ I don't make 5 prospecting calls per day

❑ I don't meet at least 5 service customers every day to prospect

❑ I have not been to the *core* skills class

❑ I don't train on JVTN® every day for at least 10 minutes

Every area you checked is an opportunity for you to improve and grow.

Even if you checked almost everything – that's OK, we have a plan.

Even if you checked everything, that's OK. If you really want to turn your job 'selling cars' into a profession, just pick any area you checked, learn more and you'll improve your unit sales and income.

Remember those Four Secrets To Success (SHAC) we talked about before? Isn't everything on these lists about your Skills, your Work Habits, your Attitude or your Choice of Customers, or a process related to one of those areas?

Exactly, and that means everything you improve on this list will take you to a new level in sales.

So follow these steps…

- If you didn't, go back and check the areas you need to work on.
- Next, circle only 3 or 4 checked boxes you'll work on *first*.
- Set an improvement goal – when will you make that change?
- Write a short plan on how you'll make the change.
- Write those 3 or 4 goals on a 3x5 card and carry it with you.
- Read your goals several times each day.
- Get to our *core selling skills* class – How To Sell A Car Today.
- Train with the chapters on JVTN® that will help you improve.
- Get to the Closing & Negotiation and Business Development classes within 90 days of attending the *core selling skills* class.

"From $60,000 per year to $112,000 with Joe Verde Training"

"I was averaging $60,000 per year before I attended my first Joe Verde Workshop 5 years ago, and I have attended 4 more workshops since then: the 2 Day Sales Workshop (twice), Closing and Negotiating Workshop, and most recently the Phone and Internet Workshop (Business Development). I sell the Joe Verde way, focusing on the customer's wants and needs. Not creating objections, but handling them and now I am averaging $112,000 per year and love my profession!" – Ford Salesperson, Brandon, MB

What do I need to do to get from 10 or 12 to 15 or 20 units?

Congratulations! If your current average is consistently above 10, you're above average and already doing a lot of things right!

I'm guessing that you're also starting to get at least *some* repeat business, and I'd guess you're getting a few of those unsold 'be-backs' back in and selling them now and then, and that you have some pretty decent presentation skills, and more closing skills than, "If I could, would you?"

The secret to get from 10 or 12 to 15 or 20 is the same as it is for the below average salesperson – you need to improve the things you aren't very good at yet. So just go back through the list and start working on the areas you checked.

> *You're selling cars and making good money.*
> *Nice job – congratulations!*

What do I need to do to improve to get past 20 or 30 units?

Here's where selling gets fun – and much easier.

If you're in the 20-30+ range now, you like sales. You're there to work, you can definitely sell, you're reasonably organized, you either follow-up and prospect or *some* customers like you enough to come back in to see you, anyway, and you either *have the goal to succeed* or you *need* the money that goes with being a high achiever.

You still have lots of areas you can improve and maintain. But for the most part, getting to your next level depends on *refining* the skills you've already developed, improving those other skills you checked, and getting better organized.

> *No matter what level you reach, to improve even more,*
> *you'll always use those same lists as a guide.*

You've read comments in here from 30, 40 and 50-car salespeople, and now it's time to start focusing on the *specific areas* that will take you to your next level, too.

✓ **Organizational Skills are HUGE to get into the 30+ unit range.**

You have to control your day better so you *can* get more done. To save time, you need a follow-up *system* instead of just 'doing' follow-up. You need a prospecting *system* and you need a *process* to automatically remind you of who to call, why you're calling and to keep that 45 / 90 day follow-up going for you.

Tip: If you're on JVTN®, start using the Virtual Sales Assistant (VSA®). It's an online CRM that I designed *just for salespeople* to control their customer base, set goals, and track everything. If you don't have JVTN®, the VSA® is at JVTN.com/vsa or you can call us – it's priced so anyone can afford it. Get it now!

✓ **Tracking everything you do is a must.**

At your level, you need to *refine* your skills even more, and to do that you have to know *exactly* what to work on. That's why you have to track every opportunity, every activity and every result you get in sales. If you're on JVTN®, use the VSA® and use our Monthly Planning Guides. Learn how to track the right way and start tracking everything you do.

No time? That's no excuse! With our planners, JVTN® and VSA®, it will take you less than 2 minutes to keep up with everything you're doing in sales. When you sell something that day, it will only take you 3 or 4 minutes extra – that's a good thing.

✓ **You need clear and specific daily goals.**

You have to focus on your priorities each day (the steps to your longer-term goals). That means you have to learn how to set goals in every area that's important in sales – and we haven't even touched on most of them yet. Goal setting, getting organized and tracking, evaluating, forecasting and charting your progress are all critical at this level in sales.

Get on JVTN® now and take the two Mini-Series we have on goal setting and getting organized. Also, go through the chapters in "How To Double Your Income Selling Cars."

✓ **Master your Phone and Internet Leads.**

All high achievers know the telephone is their secret to success in sales. If you already know how to use it pretty well, that's great and now it's time to *master* every type of call. The telephone is your most important tool to help you sell more *today* and to build a solid customer base. Get to our Business Development course so we can teach you to turn Leads and Incoming Sales Calls into appointments that show. Also, take the courses on JVTN®.

✓ **Stay focused on your critical tasks.**

We've talked about 'Traps' and mistakes, and one of the biggest mistakes high achievers make when they're busy, is they start skipping steps, especially demos and follow-up. From what we've covered, you know that skipping demos costs you sales *today.* Skipping follow-up costs you sales *tomorrow.*

Tip: Get help! There will be a point when you need someone to help you with some of the *stuff* so you can be more productive.

An assistant can make calls, schedule appointments, do your follow-up, help with paperwork when you're with a couple of customers at the same time, take a customer to service for you, and just about anything else to help free up your time so you can do what you do best (and what you get paid to do) – sell more units!

Yes, you can hope your dealer will help you, and I agree they should because you're both losing sales because you're out of time. But if they don't (my bet), that means you have two choices: get mad, simmer and lose sales or hire someone yourself. Part time college students, your (mature) kids, parents who want to work from home, your spouse, etc., can help you a ton and don't have to cost a lot. *A couple of hundred bucks a month will buy you 20 or 25 hours of part-time help, and it will make a huge difference.*

✓ **More effective Closing and Objection Handling Skills.**

Logically, being able to close and overcome objections controls your success because if there's no sale, there's no success. Get to our classes and review on JVTN®.

✓ **Improved Negotiation Skills.**

Even high achievers too often skip to price when they're busy because it *seems* faster. No matter why you talk price, it costs you sales every month, and gross on every delivery you make.

Better selling and closing skills make negotiations easier, and having more effective negotiation skills, and especially keeping the negotiation away from price and on *budget,* is the key to closing more of the deals you're writing now.

Again, class and JVTN® will help you get to your next level.

✓ **Get better at avoiding all "price" talk on the lot.**

You have to learn how to *bypass price* when it comes up early in the sale so you can focus on building value, or there won't be a sale. Then you have to learn how to *rephrase price* to budget when you're closing, so that you don't end up in a price dropping contest in the negotiation. Yep – class and JVTN®.

✓ **Stop working bell-to-bell every day.**

Work a ton in the beginning of your career to get good or when you're at your new dealership to establish your business, and then switch to working smarter. In the end, 70 and 80 hours a week will wear you down and cost you more than you're making.

Tip: Find a partner in sales like I did with my buddy Paul. We trusted each other, we were both good, we worked opposite shifts so one of us was always there, and we split more than a dozen deals each month.

✓ **Constantly improve everything you do each quarter and each year, *without exception.***

Always work on *you* and put an automatic goal setting process in place in the VSA®. Put a reminder in your phone or on your calendar to remind you every 30 to 90 days to evaluate your skills and set new improvement goals for the next year, the next quarter and for next month. And always set those activity and result goals based on your Current Average.

Congratulations – you're a sales professional – now get even better!

Skills: Your Next Step

1. Select one...

   ❏ I don't earn $100,000+, but I wish I did.

   ❏ I don't earn $100,000+, but I will in the next 12 months.

   ❏ I already earn $100,000+, and I will improve even more.

2. On the skills I need to improve...

   In this chapter, I checked off a total of ___ skills I need to work on to 1) either earn $100,000 in the next 12 months, or 2) skills that I need to work on so I can get to my next level, if I'm already earning over $100,000 a year.

3. My commitment to develop the skills I entered in #2...

   ❏ I will train on JVTN® for at least 10 minutes daily.

   ❏ I will attend the course "How To Sell A Car & Close The Sale Today" so I can develop my core selling skills.

   ❏ I will attend the course; "How To Close & Negotiate" so that I can learn to close and negotiate for more sales and maximum gross profit.

   ❏ I will attend the "Business Development" course so I can learn how to prospect, follow-up sold and unsold customers, and how to retain my customers for life, to guarantee my future growth in sales.

----

*"It's the big choices we make that set our direction.
It's the small choices we make that get us to the destination."*

– Choices

CHAPTER 12

Shortcuts To Skill Development

There's no shortcut to success or to the sale, but I'll show you how to take the only shortcut there is in selling, and that's developing your skills *faster* so you can start closing more sales *sooner.*

First let's look at the four stages of developing skills in anything we do. And then I'll give you several tips on how you can learn *more,* and learn it *faster.*

There are 4 stages of skill development…

1. Unconsciously Incompetent.

>   Example: In Boxing: I keep getting knocked out and I have no
>   idea how to fight or defend myself.

I'm not any good and I have no idea why.

This means exactly what it says: People at this level don't even
know what they don't know. These people aren't very good at their
jobs – they can't be because they don't know anything.

In fact, this pretty much describes my own skill level during my
first five years. I certainly knew *some* things about a car just from
owning them, but because we didn't get any training on how to
follow the Basics, or on how to close the sale, overcome objections,
or negotiate, I couldn't actually *sell* – and I didn't know why.

I couldn't follow-up my unsold prospects to pick up those other
8 sales most 10-car guys miss, because I didn't even know why
I should follow-up, much less how to. As for phone skills, I had
no idea what we were supposed to do, so I missed all of those
opportunities, too.

Because picking up just those 8 sales apiece from unsold follow-up
would have doubled my sales at my first dealership – I can only
assume my manager was as clueless as I was, and knew nothing
about how to teach us how to follow-up, either.

Check the key skills you really don't understand at all…

❏ Warm Up: 1st Impressions, Greeting, Rapport, Investigation
❏ Value Building: Sell Service, Evidence, Presentation, Demo
❏ Closing: Summary Close, Assumptive, Action, Final Close
❏ Objections: Bypass, Clarify, Rephrase, Isolate, Close, Refocus
❏ Negotiate: Set Up, 1st Pass, 2nd Pass Gross, 3rd Pass Wrap Up
❏ Sales Calls: Control, Expand Inventory, Appointment, Anchor
❏ Internet Leads: 1st Reply, The $, The Call, Appt., Anchor
❏ Unsold Follow-Up: T/U Note, 1st, 2nd, 3rd Call, Your System
❏ Retention: Delivery, 1st Service, 6-Step F/Up, Retention Process

2. Consciously Incompetent.

> Example: In Boxing: I'm still getting knocked out, but now I know what I need to be doing to win.

Now I know what I don't know, but I'm still not good.

Once I started reading books on selling, the 'ah, that makes sense' lights started coming on. And the more I read, the more I realized there were skills in sales I had never even thought of that would help me sell more cars, have more fun and make more money.

I didn't have the skills, but I learned what they were.

The good news is that by being *aware* of things I didn't know, it also made me *aware of the benefits* to me of developing these new skills.

Most people are serious about selling more. Becoming aware of what we don't know is generally all it takes to motivate most people to really dig in and learn how to grow and improve. In fact, who wouldn't want to develop the skills they know would help them sell more, earn more and provide more for themselves and their family?

If you've been reading this book with an open mind, you have reached this 2nd level on the skills you didn't realize that you needed to improve. Now the real work starts.

Write down the 5 most important skills you know you need and why.

1. _____
   Why? _____
2. _____
   Why? _____
3. _____
   Why? _____
4. _____
   Why? _____
5. _____
   Why? _____

3. Consciously Competent.

Example: In Boxing: My boxing skills are improving, but I'm still not responding fast enough and I still have to think about what to do. I'm still hitting the canvas now and then, but I'm winning more fights than ever.

I'm getting better but I still have to think about how to do everything I've been learning.

At this level I was learning the skills I needed in sales, but using them was still hard work because I had to really focus on everything I was saying and doing.

Because I hadn't mastered those skills yet, selling was a mental chess game as I tried to remember what I was supposed to be saying and doing each step along the way.

Even though I was selling more at this level, now I was even more aware of the sales I was missing. Why? Because now I could replay the sale in my mind, and I could spot exactly where and why I didn't make each one I missed.

What skills are you using that are working for you now – but that you know you need to improve even more?

- _____
- _____
- _____
- _____
- _____
- _____
- _____
- _____
- _____
- _____
- _____
- _____

4. Unconsciously Competent.

Example: In Boxing: I'm good, I fight instinctively now and I
am winning almost every time.

Selling is now a no-brainer and doesn't require conscious thought!

Underline the key skills in the next paragraph you've mastered.
Then go back and highlight the ones that still need improvement...
Now you can turn Internet leads into calls and into appointments
that show, answer incoming calls correctly, bypass price, and
turn them into appointments on the lot, get names & numbers
so you can follow-up the people who don't buy, make that first
follow-up call, avoid price, close on the appointment, anchor
it and have them show on the lot, prospect by phone with the
5-question referral script, work the service drive for referrals, and
when you get a customer on the lot – greet them, make a great
1st impression, bypass price, control the conversation and process,
build rapport, find their hot buttons, sell service and the dealership,
answer their questions, select the vehicle you'll send them home in,
drive first on the demo to cover FABs they care most about, give
the secondary buyer a great targeted presentation & the primary
buyer a great targeted presentation, start your closing sequence at
the landmark, use your assumptive close as you pull on the lot, get
a dozen action closes, finish it off with your final closing question,
clarify, rephrase, isolate and close again on objections they bring
up, set up the negotiation properly, start it with that 1st-pass to
pull their highest KTB numbers, 2nd-pass to go for the gross and
the 3rd-pass to wrap it up and get a bump, complete all of the
paperwork, transition it correctly to finance, make their first service
appointment before they take delivery, deliver it properly, start the
6-step follow-up process for sold customers with a thank you note,
first call, 'who's who', duplicate 'who's who', mailing list, master list,
45-day mailouts, 90-day calls and then working with the rest of the
dealership team, complete the retention process – so you can start it
all over again.

*The Catch...*after you've mastered any skill – just like the professional
boxer in these examples, you have to keep practicing everything daily
to retain your new skills.

How To Develop Your Skills Faster

There's a slow route and a faster route to developing skills. If you were to take the slow route, you could spend several years developing these skills.

Or you can take these shortcuts and spend a few days working on some of the easier skills, a few weeks on some of the mid-range skills and a few months really honing major skills until you've mastered all of them, so you can use those skills the rest of your career to sell more.

The following are the quick and easy shortcuts you can follow that will save you years of frustration and years of lost sales.

Slow down...

When you read my books, attend class or go through chapters on JVTN®, remember the goal is to learn more, not to see how fast you can get through the material. We have some people who pride themselves on having watched 500 chapters on JVTN® in a week.

I used the word 'watched' instead of taken – because you can't properly go through an 8-minute training video in 8 minutes and do the work it takes to turn the information into a skill you can use. Don't confuse quantity with quality, because when you're trying to learn more and develop skills – *speed kills.*

Retention...

You've forgotten 60% of what you read or heard just 20 minutes ago and by tomorrow, it's closer to 90% unless you work hard to retain it.

Example: Don't look them up, just answer these questions...

1. What % of the prospects who leave without buying will return with good follow-up? ___% What % will buy when they come back? ___% Understanding and doing unsold follow-up daily can just about double your sales and income. See Page 62.

2. What % of the features on your vehicles do your customers really care about? ___% (That's why you find hot buttons.) P-56

3. What % will shop price if you give it to them on the lot, on the phone or in email? ___% (That's why you learn to bypass.) P-60

See what I mean by speed reading?
The goal is to learn, not to go fast!

We learn through repetition.

If you hear or read something 6 times, you'll remember 50% of it. You'll remember even more *and be able to use* what you learn, if you put in some extra effort to develop your skills.

Don't just read or watch – develop your skills.

Reading a book or watching a video won't change your income, *applying* what you learn is the only way to do that. Your goal is to take the information you learn and turn it into a skill that you own. Developing skills takes practice, and practice, and more practice.

Some quick tips on developing your skills…

1. **Prepare yourself to retain more of what you learn.**

   Never start reading a book or start training on JVTN® without a pen, paper and a highlighter, so you can take great notes.

   Remember, you forget almost everything you hear, except what you highlight, write down and then review later.

   If you haven't already done this, go get that 3-ring binder and add notes on everything you learn, starting today. This will become *your* personal training manual.

   Create 3 main sections called: Get, Sell, and Keep.

   • Get: This section will include Unsold Follow-Up, Prospecting, Sales Calls, Internet Leads, using Social Media.

   • Sell: This section will include all of the skills in The New Basics™, Handling Price & Objections, Closing, Negotiation.

   • Keep: Include everything you learn about retaining customers; Sold Follow-Up, Retention Skills and Processes.

   All of our classes come with complete workbooks and homework books, and there are complete sets available with the four main JVTN® series on *core skills*. Add those to your 3-ring binder so you have everything in one place for easy reference.

   As you start learning more, your first binder will get too big and soon each section will need its own 3-ring binder. And every time you add pages and sections from what you're learning, your sales grow and your paychecks get bigger.

2. **Go through a video the first time to get the big picture. Then go through it as many times as it takes to develop your skills.**

Example: The Fast Start Series on JVTN® for all salespeople. It's 25 chapters, and about 3 hours in length.

How fast could you watch it? That's just math; you could watch the entire series before noon, and even take a few breaks. Not a bad idea if you're just viewing it for the first time to understand the big picture before you start developing your skills.

How fast should you go through the series though, to develop your skills? *That's a different story.*

Going through it correctly, the Fast Start Series should take you at least a week, even if you're doing it quickly. In one week, you'll develop a few good skills and you'll increase sales immediately.

Go through it *slowly* to learn all you can, though. Spend 30 to 45 days reviewing key chapters and key skills, again and again. When you've completed the Fast Start Series this way, you'll have developed solid skills that will take your selling and income average to a new and higher level right away. You'll stay at that new level as long as you keep reviewing what you learned, and as long as you keep using those new skills.

Tip: Pause after each main point to 'think it over' a little, so you really get a chance to grasp the concept.

There are more than a dozen complete series in JVTN® on the *core skills* you have to develop, some have 50+ chapters. Take your time to really understand and learn everything in there.

Pausing to absorb what we just covered is important because every BIG skill is made up of a lot of smaller skills and combined with other activities and processes. Like a book, each chapter in a series on JVTN® builds on the previous chapter and adds skills as it progresses. That means it's critical that you understand each point before you move onto the next.

Example: Sold Follow-Up is a skill, but you also have a 6-step process to learn, and you need to organize your daily activities to pull it off every day. (Don't worry – it's easy!)

3. Wear out your books, workbooks from class and JVTN®.

I have two kinds of books on my shelf; the ones in great shape because they weren't very good so I only glanced through them. Then I have the ones I've worn out from reading again and again and from taking notes in and marking up the pages.

Really use your workbooks and homework books from class and JVTN® to help you develop skills. They aren't meant to sit on a shelf. They're filled with skills, processes, activities and scripts on everything we cover in class *and then some*. They won't make you a penny sitting on the shelf or stuck in a box somewhere.

Same thing with JVTN® – except you can't wear it out. In fact, because we add new chapters and new games or role plays and mini-series all the time, it's highly unlikely you'll complete all the training, the games and role plays that are online, no matter how hard you try.

Tag your *favorites* as you go through JVTN® chapters so you can quickly find them again. Use the *key word search* to help you find a topic quick when you need it. If you have an important call to make, take a couple of minutes, use the *search* feature to find 'Sales Calls' and review 'Getting Ready To Pick Up The Phone', so you're prepared and ready to take control of the call.

Our JVTN® series cover complete processes. Most chapters in the series are in the 6-10 minute range, which is perfect for training on a time budget. Plus, if you have a Smartphone, you can even train on JVTN® while you're waiting for your appointment to show up. You can also access the VSA® on your Smartphone to add your tracking and customer information.

Treat JVTN® and our courses as a *technical manual on selling*. Pick a topic (skill) each month to focus on and then learn something about that topic every day – use my book, your class workbook, or the chapters on JVTN®. You could tag your favorites online, highlight important points, dog-ear your favorite pages in the books, and go through a video with breakfast or thumb through a chapter of my book before bed.

4. Practice and practice and practice!

There's no shortcut to turn what you learn into skills you can use. Developing skills requires a clear goal on what you want to accomplish (learn), a clear and specific plan you can follow and it takes practice and practice to develop skills.

Note: Reading this 10 times isn't practice, that's reading it 10 times. Saying the words out loud is part of practicing. Focusing on your tone and inflection and delivery is part of practice, and having someone role play with you is part of practicing.

5. Evaluate and chart your skill level!

After you've taken or read a chapter, and after you've reviewed your notes, evaluate yourself on that topic every 30 to 60 days. Use a 1–10 rating and chart the numbers. Why? Because when you're focusing on a skill, your ratings will go up. When you stop focusing on a skill, they'll likely drop. A regular rating schedule will help keep your skills in tip-top shape.

6. Focus on your potential to stay pumped!

In your notes, rate your potential for improvement. How many more units could you see yourself selling this month *if* you improved your skills, or improved your habits or your attitude in that area?

You'll be shocked at how quickly your sales potential builds as you learn more. Be realistic – don't highball yourself and fill in these three guesstimates…

1. How many more units would you sell if you improved, and then gave every person a better demonstration? ___

2. How many more units would you sell right now if you did your follow-up with every unsold prospect? ___

3. How many more units would you sell right now if you knew more ways to close the sale? ___

   Make a commitment to learn more and let's make this the first day of your brand new career in sales!

Why Is Daily Training Critical?

Spring was in the air and the annual wood chopping contest was the final event of the County Fair. The crowds gathered, the excitement grew as the two finalists were about to begin. One man was the reigning champion, the hometown favorite and had won the contest year after year. The other was a new guy in his first contest. All of the odds were on the bigger, and more experienced reigning champion.

The challenge was to see who could chop the most wood in one hour. Both men readied their axes, the starter fired the shot and the contest began. Trees fell, chips flew and wood was piling up.

But about 20 minutes into the contest the new guy asked the champ if it would be OK for him to take a short break. The crowd was shocked, our champion laughed and was all for it, thinking 'what an idiot', while he just kept chopping and chopping.

After another 20 minutes or so, the new guy asked the champ if he'd mind if he took another short break. Again, completely sure of his win, the champ said, "Sure, take as long as you want."

The one-minute warning came as both men chopped as fast as possible, the final bell rang and the champion held his axe high in the air with no doubt in his mind he'd won, especially with the new guy taking breaks throughout the contest.

The judges counted the wood, handed their scorecards to the ring master who grabbed the microphone and said, "Ladies and Gentlemen – the judges have reached a unanimous decision. The winner of the 44th annual wood chopping contest is … the new guy!"

The crowds quietly cheered as they looked on in amazement and the champion was shocked. As the announcer interviewed the new guy he asked, "I'm sure everyone in the audience and our 12-time champ has the same question. How in the world did you win, especially since you took two breaks?"

The new guy said …

"I wasn't actually taking a break, I was sharpening my axe."

Once most salespeople even come close to mastering a skill, they tend to stop focusing on improving themselves. And the one truism about skills is like the axe; if you don't take the time to continue your education to keep every one of your skills sharp – soon they won't be.

What Will You Do Daily
To Develop Your Skills & Keep Them Sharp?

1. I will continually work on one of these 3 major skills every day...

   • _____

   • _____

   • _____

2. To make sure I work on my skills daily, I will...

   • _____

   • _____

   • _____

   • _____

   • _____

Remember:
If you'll work harder than anybody else will for 5 years,
you'll earn more than anybody else can the rest of your life.

"I went from 4.5 to 13.5 from reading your book."

"I've been in the car business for almost 3 years. I was averaging 4-½ a month, barely getting by and I knew I had to make changes, so I got your book, 'How to Sell a Car Today'.

Reading your book was a life changing experience. Since then my average has gone up to 13-½! Thanks, Joe." Lowell, Nissan, TN

CHAPTER 13

Using Goals
To Manage Your Career

If you learn more, develop more skills and go to work to work, you'll earn twice what the average person selling cars today earns.

But $80,000 a year isn't $100,000 and that should just be your first goal – not your ultimate goal. But we're running out of book here and we still have to talk about how to pull all of this together and make it happen.

So to get you over $100,000, in the next three chapters we need to cover the "Success Skills" you'll need to improve now, and to grow year after year...

Goal Setting – Tracking – Getting Organized

Goal Setting

In general, what is a goal?

A goal is something you want to have or something you want to do now or in the future. A goal can be just about anything from a simple task, to the most challenging things you'll do in business or life.

Which of these are goals?

❏ Read this book.

❏ Earn $100,000 in the next 12 months.

❏ Send someone a birthday card.

❏ Give 75% of your customers a demo this month.

❏ Get your kids to the soccer game at 5:30.

❏ Average 30 units per month at 75% repeat business within 6 mo.

❏ Pick up milk and eggs at the grocery store.

Of course, they're all goals. Some seem like they're no-brainers and some will take elaborate planning. But if you stop and think about it, you don't even read a book accidentally. Almost everything you do is a goal in one form or another.

Bigger Goals...

Some goals listed above are not 'no-brainers'. You may get lucky and remember to pick up the eggs, but 'Earning $100,000 Per Year' will not just happen. That goal will take more elaborate planning, and you'll have to combine multiple *activities* to make it happen.

Who do you think uses goals to help them grow?

❏ The most successful people

❏ The least successful people

Exactly, common sense says the *most successful people are the goal setters*. Sure, some big things happen accidentally, like being in your rich uncle's will. That wasn't about goal setting – it just happened. But *accidental success* isn't what we're talking about here. Like I said earlier in the book, you can get lucky and make $10,000 one month, but you don't get lucky and earn $100,000 per year.

What facts do we know about goal setting?

When we talk about setting goals, we know...

1. 87% of the people have no goals at all (other than those daily activity goals like picking up the milk and eggs).

    This doesn't mean they don't want to be more successful, or they don't work very hard to try to become successful or to accomplish something special.

    This fact just means that 87% of all the people don't set goals.

2. 10% of the people sorta have goals, but they don't do it right.

    There are rules to goal setting, and these 10%'ers are trying even harder to hit their goals, but they didn't follow the rules.

    You can keep repeating, "I want to earn over $100,000 this year," until your voice wears out, but if you don't have a written goal, a written plan and then if you don't do all the activities it takes to make it happen, even luck won't help.

3. 3% of the people set goals the right way (and I'll explain that in just a minute).

    Here are a couple of extra facts we know about these 3%'ers:

    a. The 3% who do set goals *correctly,* will earn 10 times as much money in their lifetimes as non-goal setters.

    b. The 3% who do set goals *correctly,* have more money than the other 97% combined.

So if these are the facts about goal setters, and you want to earn over $100,000 every year you sell cars, what do you need to do? Exactly, you need to learn how to set goals the right way.

I think I just heard somebody say, "Everything isn't all just about the money, Joe." Of course it isn't. Money is just what these stats focus on. But if we look at it logically, and only 3% set goals correctly for the money, then it's logical to also assume only 3% set goals correctly for just about every other goal in life, too.

A Goal:
A dream with a deadline!

How big should your goals be?

You want to think big and you always want to stretch yourself so you can grow. But you don't want to stretch your imagination to a point that you know you can't hit (at least not yet). These two famous men give you the guidelines on goal setting...

Henry Ford – *"Whether you think you can, or can't, you'll be right."*

Napoleon Hill – *"When you can see it and believe it, you can achieve it."*

And we've all heard – *"What you see, is what you get."*

So the answer on how big goals should be...

Goals need to be realistic and achievable.

And there's only one person who can make that decision: YOU.

If you set small goals and consistently hit or exceed them, through experience you'll learn how to win with goal setting. If you set big goals and consistently miss them, through experience you'll learn two things: how to fail with goal setting, and how to come up with a list of reasons to explain why it isn't your fault you never win.

Always stretch yourself – but not your imagination.

What kinds of goals do you need?

There are *results* goals – the things you want to accomplish, like getting a new house, or being number one in sales, or earning $100,000 next year. Then there are *activity* goals, and those are the things you'll have to do to reach your *results* goals. And we'll cover more *result and activity goals* in a few minutes.

Are you ready for the trade?

Here's what holds most people back – the trade they have to make to hit their goals. What trade? Actually there are quite a few.

If you want to earn $100,000, you certainly can, but not without paying a price. You'll have to give up some TV time to train on JVTN® instead, you'll have to 'go to work to work' and walk away from the huddle to make some calls, and you'll have to trade a few days of your life to attend our three 2-day classes on how to sell a car today, close and negotiate and how to build your business.

It's so easy to justify not making those trades – the 10 minutes to watch JVTN®, the money it takes to attend 3 classes, the 6 days away from the dealership, the sales you'll miss, and, and, and. There are always reasons not to – but here's what most people don't consider.

Which do you prefer, one million or two million?

Everybody will earn a million dollars – the only question is how long it will take. If you earn $50,000 / year now, that's $4,166 per month and if you keep that up, in the next 20 years, you'll earn $1,000,000 selling cars. That's an above-average income, so congratulations.

If you attend our 3 classes (6 days total), and use JVTN® to train for just 8 to 10 minutes per day, and go to work to work – you'll hit your $100,000 per year goal, and continue to improve year after year.

Earning $100,000 per year is $8,333 per month, which means you'll earn *at least* $2,000,000 selling cars in the next 20 years. That's a *minimum,* because once you start setting clear goals and once you start receiving the benefits, most people never stop improving.

The point is – you have a choice to make. Like it or not, you're going to work every day for the next 20 years (7,300 days). So you have to *choose one option right now* that will affect your income and your family's lifestyle for the next 20 years. *Putting off* this choice is not an option. Putting off your decision simply defaults to 'doing nothing different'. The clock is ticking, so will you...

❑ Do nothing different, justify why you won't bother, and only earn $50,000 per year / $1 Million in the next 20 years?

❑ Spend just 6 of those next 7,300 days to attend class, and then spend just 10 minutes per day studying on JVTN® to improve and earn $100,000 / $2 Million for you and your family instead?

The crummy part of reading "Choices" – it reminds you that *once you become aware of an option – it becomes a conscious choice.* Now if you don't say, "Yes, I will" – your choice defaults to – "No, I won't."

If you're still unsure it's worth it to make an extra million, just go home, and say, "Honey, I just learned how I could double my income and earn an extra million dollars in the next 20 years, plus I'd end up working fewer hours – do you think I should do it?"

How do you set goals the right way?

This is a big question for such a short chapter, so let's cover as much as we can. *Here are some basic rules to goal setting...*

1. First, goals have to be realistic and achievable.

   I'm never the one to say people can't reach any goal because there are so many examples of people being able to pull off the impossible – when it's important to them.

   At the same time, I believe realistic means 'practical'. Is it possible that a salesperson selling 8 units now could sell 50 units if he had a goal? Absolutely, we've seen it happen.

   • Is it realistic that he'll sell 50 next month? Not really.

   • Is it realistic to hit 50 per month within a year? Yes.

   • Is it realistic to hit 50 as a 5-year goal? It's a piece of cake.

   Time and effort are usually the difference between realistic and unrealistic. Invest more time and effort to learn and develop skills faster, and more effort in daily activities that will lead to hitting the goal – and you can shorten the goal time frame.

2. Improvement goals have to be based on facts, not guesstimates.

   If you sell 15 units now, is getting from 15 to 20 next month pretty easy? Sure. Is getting from 8 units to 20 next month as realistic? Not so easy and not very likely, unless there's a solid plan and consistent effort to hit the goal.

   One of the biggest problems in setting production and activity goals is that salespeople don't track what they do, so they don't know their starting point. So most tend to use their best months as the answer when asked, "How many cars do you sell?"

   We'll cover tracking in a few pages, but remember this thought about tracking and your future success:

   Tracking is the single most important
   thing that salespeople, managers and dealers
   don't do – when it comes to continuous improvement.

3. 94% of (realistic) written goals are achieved.

    A lot of people think just telling themselves 'I'm going to make $100,000 this year' is all it takes. They don't understand how the process works. *Please don't argue, just write your goals down.*

    To learn how to set effective goals...

    • Step 1...Sit down with a pen and paper and just make a list of everything you'd like to have or do. *And for now*, leave out the words *realistic and achievable*. Just go for it. List anything and everything you can think of you want to have, do or be. If you do this right, you should fill a page or two.

    • Step 2...After you make that giant list, go through each thing on your list and beside each item, rate it as a 1, 2 or 3.

    The 1's will be the priority items on your list – things you for sure want to accomplish.

    The 2's will be the things that you'd like to do or have at some point in your life, but they aren't priorities now.

    The 3's are just things on your 'wish list' that fall into the 'wouldn't it be great to have' category.

    • Step 3...Now go back and date the 1's, those priority items on your list. You'll turn them into goals *with a date to achieve that goal.* The date is critical.

    Why this process? Because psychologists tell us by the time we're 6 or 7 years old, 80% of us have all but lost our imagination. We've heard so many of those *be careful, don't do this, you can't do that,* and *you'll never be able to's* that we've forgotten how to dream big. This process will help you fire up your imagination again, and that's critical to your growth.

    They also said the younger you are, the more things you'll have on the list above, and as we get older, we'll have fewer. This is proven in our classes when we assign this homework. The next day, we see real long lists from the younger people – the older people generally have only 2 or 3 things on their lists. That's too bad, because we need our imagination to help us stretch ourselves with goals. *Practice dreaming BIG.*

4. Leave out the "failure options" when you set goals.

Reaching goals requires making a *commitment to yourself.*

• Is this a priority?

• Do I believe I can actually pull it off?

• Am I willing to make a total commitment to hit the goal?

Too many people who set goals have so little real *desire* to reach their goals, and / or so little real *confidence* in themselves being able to reach the goal, and / or so little *determination* to dig deep enough to do the work it takes to make it happen, they shouldn't even waste their time pretending they set goals.

"I'm going to earn $100,000 in the next twelve months, unless something happens," or "I'm going to do my best to make this happen," or "I'll sure try," are all things people say to give themselves an out when they don't hit the goal.

Leave out the *unless*, *best shot*, and *try*, and just set a goal that's realistic and important enough for you to say, "I will."

Will You 'Do It'...or... Will You 'Try It'?

An expedition was organized to climb the north wall of the Matterhorn; which had never been done. So reporters interviewed members of the team who were from around the world.

A reporter asked one man, "Are you going to climb the north wall?" The man replied, "I'm going to give it everything I have."

The reporter asked a second member, "Are you going to climb the north wall of the Matterhorn?" The climber answered, "I'm going to do the very best I can."

Still another was asked if he was going to climb the north wall and he said, "I'm going to give it my very best effort."

The reporter asked another young man, "Are you going to climb the north wall?" This man looked him dead center and said, "I will climb the north wall of the Matterhorn."

Only one man succeeded – the one who said, "I will!"

---

5. Set Result & Activity Goals ... You have to learn how to set and reach two kinds of goals; result *and* activity goals.

   Your result goal is what you want to happen, the '$100,000'. Your activity goals are what you'll have to do to hit your results goal. These activity goals become your *written plan.*

   If you just say, "I'm going to make $100,000" ... good luck! On the other hand, if you write out a clear *results goal* with a deadline like: "I will earn over $100,000 in the next 12 months (or by __/__)", and then create a detailed plan that includes the *activity goals* you'll also have to accomplish to hit your *results* goal, get ready to *reach and exceed* your goal.

   A goal only takes a sentence – but your plan will take the rest of the page. To hit your $100,000 *results goal*, a list of your primary *activity goals* would look a lot like this...

   - Rate all of my skills in the previous chapter
   - Get to Joe's sales classes to develop my skills
   - Train daily on JVTN® for a minimum of 10 minutes to improve a skill I'll need to reach my goal
   - Practice my selling scripts for at least 20 minutes each day
   - Go to work to work every day and stay out of the huddle
   - Call 5 previous customers and 5 orphan owners, and use the 5 question referral prospecting script
   - Meet 5 service customers a day and use the referral script
   - Make firm appointments on 60% of my incoming sales calls
   - Demo 75% of the people I talk to each month
   - Get a firm commitment to buy (write-up) 75% of my demos
   - Close and deliver 50% of my write-ups
   - Get 100% CSI and put every sold customer into a Master List in the VSA® and follow the 45/90 retention plan Joe teaches
   - Get 75% contact info and follow-up every unsold prospect
   - Track, average and chart all of my opportunities, activities and results so I can stay on track and set new goals regularly

   You could add more to this list, but if you only do what's here,
   you <u>will</u> earn $100,000 in the next 12 months!

6. Review your goals.

   How do we learn new things and how do we really tune into hitting our goals? Through repetition. That's the other reason you write your goals down – so you can review them regularly.

   Keep a goal list with you at all times. Write them on a business card. Keep it in your pocket and you'll accidentally remember to read them a few times each day. Set automatic reminders in your phone so they pop up at different times each day. But do something to help you review your goals every day.

   Big Tip: Set your goals in the VSA® at the beginning of each month, enter all of your daily tracking information (it takes 32 seconds) and the VSA® will keep a summary of your daily activities and give you *accurate projections* every day of where you are and what you need to do to hit your goals.

7. Set new goals every quarter, every month, every day.

   Using your *current average*, at the beginning of each new quarter you need to set three goals. Assuming you're at 14 now, here's some easy math without many fractions...

   • At the beginning of the quarter, if you're averaging 14, *how many units do you want to average one year from now?*

   • If you are at 14 units now and your twelve month goal is to average 26 units, that's 12 more units. So you need to average 17 by the end of this quarter. (1/4 of your goal.)

   • If raising your average by 3 units to hit 17 is your first quarterly goal, how many do you need to average by the end of this month? Right – 1st month raise your average to 15, next month 16, and 17 by the end of the 3rd month.

   Now each quarter, just keep repeating this goal setting process. Start with a 12 month goal, divide by 4 to get your quarterly goal. Divide quarterly by 3 to get monthly. Keep doing the math and you'll have weekly and daily *results* goals. Then when we get into *tracking*, you'll set your daily, weekly, monthly, and quarterly *activity* goals to hit your *results* goals.

   You don't need anyone else's approval. Just set your result and activity goals and go for it. You can accomplish anything!

Your First Goal List

To help you get started with your goal list, take a break and just make a quick list of 6 things you'd like to do. Do a one-year goal and a five-year goal in each group. Be realistic.

In Units...

I will deliver _____ units by __ / __ / __ (1 year from today)

I will deliver _____ units by __ / __ / __ (5 year goal)

In Income...

I will earn $____,____,____ by __ / __ / __ (1 year from today)

I will earn $____,____,____ by __ / __ / __ (5 year goal)

Other...

I will also _____

_____ by __ / __ / __

I will also _____

_____ by __ / __ / __

See how easy goal setting can be?

The goal is the easy part. It takes seconds to set a goal and just one or two sentences to put it in writing.

Now the work starts. Grab another sheet of paper *for each goal.* Write your goal at the top of a page, and then make a list of the things you'll need to do or improve on to hit each goal.

Even if you're in a hurry, make a commitment to set one goal in each area, and make your plan for that goal – today.

When you wish upon a star,
makes no difference who you are.
(As long as you set a clear goal
and write out an action plan.)

CHAPTER 14

Tracking Your
Opportunities – Activities – Results

Guesstimates don't work in goal setting. To set clear goals, you have to know *exactly* what you're doing now.

Tracking comes before goal setting, and I would have put tracking before the goals chapter, but so many people misunderstand what tracking involves, and have so much mis-information about tracking and its value, that you probably would have skipped this chapter.

If the chapter on goal setting made sense, hopefully you'll be willing to learn more about tracking now, because you can't set clear, realistic and achievable goals if you don't track what you're doing.

Tracking
(Counting Things)

I have no idea where I learned about tracking. Maybe in the leadership courses I took in the Army or from keeping maintenance logs when I worked on helicopters, maybe it was from watching football and hearing them rattle off stats about each player, or it could have been in one of the 100 plus books I read on selling and success.

I'm not sure who should get the credit, but I can't thank them enough for making me understand the critical importance of tracking everything we do in sales and using tracking to grow.

After growing up on a farm, I've always been a hard worker, and since I started *tracking* my income in 1965, there have only been 3 years I did not have a record year in my sales and income personally, and in my businesses.

I have learned how to grow <u>every year</u> – and you can too.

Growth is a really simple process:

1. Track (count) everything that happens in sales, and then find your current average so you know exactly what you're doing.
2. Set a clear goal for improvement based on your averages.
3. Develop new skills and habits to improve in that area.
4. Keep learning and practicing so you maintain your new level.
5. Start over again at #1.

There's way more to learn about how tracking can help you than I can cover in just a few pages here. So we have a one-hour session you can watch on JVTN® if you're a subscriber, and if you aren't a subscriber (yet), you can watch it FREE at JVTN.com/salesmpg.

The session is on how to use our Monthly Planning Guides, which are about 1/3 tracking, 1/3 daily planning and 1/3 managing your sold and unsold prospects. You'll want to watch the video to help with tracking, and to help with the daily planning and organization skills we'll be covering in the next chapter.

Tracking isn't complicated, and it isn't time consuming.
But it is the very first, and single most important step in growth.
It's simple – if you don't track, you can't grow (consistently)!

The goal, at least the focus of this book, is on how you can start earning $100,000 per year, every year. To get you there, and keep you at those levels, you have to track three things...

1) Track Your Opportunities

You have to know exactly how many people you talk to through email, on the phone, in person, in service and on the lot. Those are called 'opportunities' to do business. Why do you need to know? So you know where and how to improve.

For example...Let's say you take two of those incoming sales calls per day, and they turn into one delivery per week.

Some quick facts about those incoming callers...

40	Incoming sales calls (you get 2 a day x 20 work days)
90%	Buy within 1 week of calling
36	Buyers of the 40 who call about a vehicle
– 4	Deliveries
32	Who will still buy – somewhere else

It's obvious there is an opportunity to improve, but how? What do you need to do differently to deliver more of these callers?

Let's say you tracked everything this month and these are your stats...

40	Incoming sales calls
20	Appointments you made (50% of calls)
8	Shows (40% of your appointments actually came in)
4	Deliveries (you delivered 50% of shows)

Looking at the number, what do you need to do to sell more? You're pretty close to average on appointments, but you're way below average for getting them to show for their appointment.

So what skill do you need to focus on to improve your 'shows' (and deliveries)? Exactly, you have to improve your appointment skills; correctly bypassing price, getting control, repeating the appointment multiple times, anchoring it, changing it to the quarter hour, confirming your appointment, etc.

If you improve your skills and become <u>average</u>, you'll sell 75% more...

40   Incoming sales calls

24   Appointments (60% is average)

14   Shows (60% of appointments show on average)

7   Deliveries (50% of shows buy on average)

You improved your deliveries 75% without taking more calls. Now if you learn more and get even *better than average*, here is what you can expect from those same 40 incoming sales calls...

40   calls

30   appointments (75%)

22   show (75%)

13   close (60%)

From delivering 4 each month to 13 instead is a 225% increase in sales, and you did it by tracking to find your weakness and then improving your skills to *just above average.*

That's 9 more deliveries than you were getting from the same number of calls. *Improve your skills – improve your income.*

The key to tracking opportunities is to count them 'by type'.

What does that mean – by type? Remember the 'types' of buyers we talked about in Chapter 6 – walk-ins, repeats, etc.

Your real success is in the details. If you develop your *skills* and manage your *activities* to focus on more of your hottest prospects that close at 60% – you can talk to just 50 people per month and deliver 30 of them a vehicle. (Read that again.)

Every month you want to know your *current average* in...

• 'Ups' you took on the lot	• Repeat customers you brought in
• Referrals you got by phone	• Outside prospects you brought in
• Be-backs you got back in	• Dealership customers (parts / service)
• Phone ups you got on the lot	• Internet leads you brought in

If you will track every category I will talk about,
you can manage your sales and income the rest of your career.

2) Track Your Activities

This is what you did to generate a lead or a sale: Prospecting calls, follow-up calls, emails, appointments you made, appointments that show, the number of people you talked to in service, plus demos and write-ups are all things you do to either bring in a prospect, or to make a sale.

• *Prospecting Activities*...If you make those 5 prospecting calls per day we talked about before, here's what you can expect...

  100   calls per month (5 per day x 20 days)

   30   have a family member who'll trade in 90 days (30%)

   18   will make appointments (60%)

   11   will show (60%)

    7   deliver (close 60% of referrals & outside prospects)

I'm betting this activity also more than doubled your sales. All just from tracking, and then improving the related skills (control, 5-question referral script, appointment skills) and by improving your daily habits to make these 5 prospecting calls.

• *Unsold Activities*...Track the sales you miss from the people you didn't sell, and improve your skills and daily follow-up habits. Here's what we know will happen when you talk to 3 or 4 people per day (3 x 25 days = 75, but we'll use 70 for easy math)...

   70   people you talk to on the lot on *average* each month

   10   sales you make now

   60   didn't buy from you

   45   you got contact info for, of those who didn't buy (75% of 60)

   15   of 45 come back in (33% come back with good follow-up)

   10   buy on the spot when they come back (67%)

What skills did you have to develop to pick up 10 sales? Unsold follow-up, controlling the call, bypassing price, and closing on an appointment. What habits? Getting the info and making the calls.

Knowing where to focus is critical, because between incoming sales calls, prospecting calls, and following up with your unsold prospects, you can more than triple your sales and income. Wow!

3) Track Your Results

The final areas you want to track and average will be your results: Your total sales and income by type of customer. Example...

- Walk-in   Units: 3   Average $ Per: $125
- Repeat Customer   Units: 5   Average $ Per: $455
- Referrals   Units: 3   Average $ Per: $380
- Dealership (Serv.)   Units: 2   Average $ Per: $390
- Calls / Leads   Units: 2   Average $ Per: $280

Why track these? Look again. These are your results by *customer type*, so if you're trying to sell more units and make more money, which type of customer should you focus your attention on?

If these were your stats, what should you focus on every day? Would you spend your day waiting for an 'up' when you can start doing 75% of your business with the other groups *within 90 days*?

What are current averages, and why use them?

Current averages are your last 3 months' totals, divided by 3.

Why only 3 months? If this is your 12 month sales history below, *circle the 3 numbers that most accurately describe your actual performance today...*

     Last Year   Now

22 – 9 – 13 – 11 – 19 – 8 – 12 – 9 – 15 – 8 – 8 – 8

That 22 car month was great, and a 12 unit average for the last year may sound great, too, but neither number has anything to do with what's going on today in your career, because you're stuck at 8. If you'll focus on *current history*, you can easily plan growth.

This is such a non-event as far as *tough* things go. If you'll use the VSA® included in JVTN®, in just 32 seconds you'll drop in your numbers for the day, and the system does the work. And then each and every day, you'll know your averages on everything you do.

If you'll start tracking all of your opportunities, activities and results, you can finally start managing your career in sales.

From Joe's Monthly Planning Guide For Salespeople
Planning And Tracking Are Easy
(Just Fill In The Blanks)

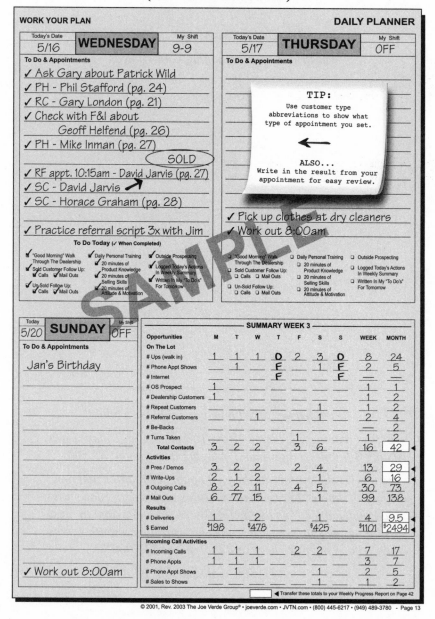

You can't manage your career
until you start managing your choices.

"I tripled my take home pay with Joe's book!"

"Before reading your book 'How To Sell A Car Today' I was selling 8-9 units a month and bringing home about $3,500.

I've read it three times in the past couple of months and now, selling is simple: I present the features and benefits Joe's way and handle objections on the lot. When it comes time to close, assuming the sale now just comes natural. Last month I more than tripled my pay check and took home $12,000!"

– Jim, Salesperson, Ford, GA

CHAPTER 15

Organization Is Critical
To Becoming A High Achiever

We've talked about your potential, gone through the stats and the skills you need so you know where to focus and spelled out the traps you need to avoid. And if you'll follow the directions and do those things, you should be on your way to that $100,000 plus income.

The only catch now is being able to get through your days more effectively so you *can* sell more units.

I absolutely got hung up between 18 and 20 units, and I couldn't seem to get out of my own way. I was either bogged down selling something, or helping a customer in service or chasing paperwork or a dozen other things.

Then I got organized. When I did, I doubled my sales and my income, and you can, too.

Getting Organized To Sell More Cars

We all know the drill on a day in sales...

- Delivering the vehicles
- Getting contracts resigned
- Chasing paperwork on deals
- Getting accessories installed in service
- Taking phone ups, answering Internet leads
- Making follow-up calls and sending out mailouts
- If you aren't careful – everything *but* selling more units

Getting organized is definitely not a skill or habit that comes to you in a dream one night, just because you sell cars for a few years. But professionals in sales know they have to organize their time so they can use every minute of the day effectively to make things happen.

I was going crazy because I knew I could sell more, but I couldn't figure out how to get everything done. Then we got a computer and my wife got my days organized. We didn't have my sales software back then so I used 3x5 cards, which are a nightmare once you *really* get into follow-up and prospecting.

Soon I created a planner to help me with my daily 'to-do' list, my appointments, my tracking, goal setting and my monthly sales summary and charts – and with all that help, I doubled my sales.

The organizer / planner I created for myself back then, grew into our paper Monthly Planning Guides, and our online salesperson's CRM, the Virtual Sales Assistant® that's included in JVTN®.

Tracking and daily planning saved me...

I finally stopped using scraps of paper to manage my career. I developed a planner for all of my tasks like 'prospecting calls' and appointments, and my own goal setting and planning pages, and I included tracking for everything we just covered. Then in just minutes each day, I managed my calls and contacts, and tracked all of my selling 'opportunities', 'activities' and 'results'.

Most people don't want to use the CRM their dealership has because it's too complicated. That's why I created our VSA® in JVTN®. It's simple, easy, and it's included with JVTN® because you have to track what you're doing so you know what to train on.

You can get a free 30-day password for the VSA® to see how it works, and you can view a sample planner online, too, so you can get an idea of how they work and what you need to track. But whether you use my planners and VSA® or try to create your own, here are some of the things you have to figure out how to do in sales.

At the beginning of the month...

Monthly Forecasting, Planning & Goal Setting.

Using your tracking and current averages from last month, you'll plan your sales and income for this month. If you're averaging 10 units and earning $3,000, you earn $300 per unit.

You'll always use your *current averages* to set your goals. Using current averages, you know if you just keep doing what you're doing, you'll sell 10 and make $3,000. But this month your goal is to deliver 12, and to increase your commission per unit to $350.

Your unit goal is 12 – but since you also set a goal to increase your gross and commission, what is your income goal? Exactly; 12 units x $350 (your new per unit goal) = $4,200

Now what's the plan? How will you sell 2 more units and raise your commissions $50? It's back to the tracking for the answers.

- Look at your incoming call *show* and *closing* averages. If you close 50%, get four more 'shows', you'll sell two more units.

- How about demos? We know 50% buy on the spot when they get a good one – so up your demos by 4, and you'll sell 2 more.

- What about the gross? Well, if you're on 25%, to increase your commission $50 you'll need to raise the gross $200. How? Stay off price and build more value (those extra demos will help).

- Hedge your bet by making at least 2 prospecting calls per day.

  Now just turn these into goals with plans you follow daily.

Your Daily Planning...

• Part of your daily planning will be to make sure you do the *activities* we just outlined so you can sell 2 units and raise the gross.

Your *Action Plan* items will become your daily 'to-do' items...

– Call two prospects and ask for referrals

– Give everyone a demonstration today (or 36 demos this month)

– Stay off price and build value

– Watch one JVTN® chapter on bypassing price

– Watch one JVTN® chapter on demonstrations

• Your other daily to do items will include things like...

– Your dentist appointment at 5

– Bob & Betty Smith appointment at 3 today

– Verify Smith appointment at noon

• You also have your tracking information (numbers) to fill in each day. Here again, if you're using the planners or the VSA®, you'll just write in or type in your number.

So you really understand how long it takes to do this *each day*, just write the numbers I put in below in the blanks to the right of them. Use your stop watch to see how long it takes.

'Ups'	1	_____
Repeat	1	_____
Referrals	1	_____
Demos	3	_____
Write-Ups	2	_____
Sales	2	_____
Commissions	$500	$_____
Incoming calls	2	_____
Appointments	2	_____

Seriously – fill in the blanks and time yourself so you really do understand just how <u>not</u> difficult tracking is. All you have to do is just count your 'ups' etc., and then enter that number each day.

- *Your Working Prospects*...These are the people you're working with now to try to get them in to sell a vehicle. They could be new prospects, previous customers or someone from service.

  You need to get away from the scraps of paper and the backs of business cards approach to managing your working prospects.

  In the planner and the VSA® you'll enter every new contact you met on the lot with their contact information and information about the vehicle they're interested in, trade information, etc.

  Because you're entering information in your planner *and* the VSA® or your CRM at work, when you go home you'll take your planner with you, so no matter where you are, you'll have everything you need to manage your customer contacts. Plus, if you're on JVTN® and have a SmartPhone, you'll also have access to your tracking and <u>all of your contacts</u>, there, too.

- *Your Sold Customers*...Once you make the sale to a new prospect or someone you've been working, you'll just change the status from 'working' to 'sold' in the VSA®, and transfer the customer info into your planner in the 'Monthly Sales Log'.

  Your Monthly Sales Log is one of the most important sections in your planner / VSA® because here's where you identify your 'customer type' information we talked about. This not only becomes your central source for all of your sales, this becomes a permanent record of who, what, when and how much you earned every day. You'll want to keep your planners forever.

  Just circle the customer type, enter the source (how you or the dealership generated this sale), whether the vehicle was new or pre-owned, and how much you earned in commission and bonus.

  At the end of the month, the math is automatic in the VSA®, and because it's already organized in the planner, it's almost that easy, too. Just grab a calculator and add the columns and you'll know everything you need to know to start managing your business.

How long does it really take to log your to-do's, appointments, working prospects and enter your tracking and sales? 3 to 5 minutes.

So far, we've only used a few minutes of your day,
and you're totally organized and ready to be productive.

At the end of the month...

- Your End Of Month Summary...Now it's time to summarize all of these numbers you've been dropping into the planner or VSA® so you can find those current averages we talked about.

  In the VSA®, it's all automatic. In fact, at any time during the month, you can pull up your reports and know exactly where you're at for the month, and exactly where that will put you at the end of the month. You'll have averages, charts and graphs in almost every category we've talked about in here.

  In the Monthly Planner, it's all automatic, too, right after you manually do the math and create your charts. Just kidding, but if you're using both, you'll just copy the information from the VSA® to the planner. Why bother transferring the information? Because it will only take you a minute or two and you'll have a permanent record. The planners come 3-hole punched and should be put into a yearly 3-ring binder that you keep forever.

  I know this sounds like a little bit of trouble. But just remember the goal. We're talking about earning over $100,000 a year for the rest of your career, and there is some important paperwork that goes along with earning that kind of income.

- Once your end-of-month paperwork is done (in about 10 minutes or less), it's time to start planning next month – so grab your new Monthly Planning Guide, turn to the 'forecasting, planning and goal setting' section – and start all over.

"But Joe, this all sounds too easy. That's not what the 6-car guy told me about tracking and being organized – is it really this easy?"

The only reason this will take longer, will be when you start selling more. So in real life, *you should hope you get buried* in having to enter more sold customer information every day.

Can all of this training, tracking and getting organized work for you, too? I got an email from a salesperson who came to our classes and has been on JVTN® since the day we released it. His email...

"Joe – Before I attended your Sales Class, I was selling 12 units and last month I delivered 38." – Nick, Salesperson, Ford

I called Nick and we talked about how he got from 12 to 38 and it was by doing everything we're talking about in here. As we talked about improving even more, it was obvious he could *sell,* and he wanted to know what he'd need to do to move into the 50 and 60 unit per month range.

At those levels, it's all in the details, and getting more organized was what he and I talked about. Just like when I got stuck, his skills weren't his problem, his biggest challenge was being organized enough each day so he could talk to more people and *use* his skills.

Did it work? Did Nick go back and apply what we talked about? Absolutely. He's a pro and wasn't just asking me what I thought just to get my opinion – he wanted to improve and grow.

Nick's next update...

"Joe – About a year ago, I told you I'd gone from selling 12 units to 38 units after attending your workshops. Here's my newest update: Last month, I delivered 50 units."
– Nick, Salesperson, Ford

High Achievers Manage Their Careers

Here's a real quick story about another high achiever who manages her day effectively so she can get in, and get back out of the dealership and work decent hours, while she still makes big bucks.

I was in our Leadership course and one of the General Managers told me about one of his salespeople who'd been to our training. She had been to class, improved to 26 units per month and then came to another class and improved even more, just like Nick did.

Because I already knew about her success and how much she'd improved, I told the GM I'd bring her results up in class, and asked him to tell the class about her so they could hear it from him, not me.

I told everyone she'd come to class and got to 26 units and then came back to class again.

I asked the GM..."*So how's she doing now?*"

Her GM said..."*Her new current average is 42 units.*"

Again, I already knew the story but I really wanted him to make the next point. So I asked, "*WOW – she must be working bell-to-bell, 7 days a week to pull that off, huh?*"

His reply..."*No, she only works from 8 to 5, Monday through Friday.*"

> *Success isn't about how much time you spend at work;*
> *Productivity comes from what you do while you're at work!*

One last thought about being organized...

Distractions are one of the biggest problems to deal with when you're trying to get through an effective day selling. When I started selling again, I'd be doing my follow-up or prospecting, and the other salespeople kept coming in to hang around and talk.

Once they realized I wasn't going to stop working to visit with them, they stopped coming by, but not before they told me how I had become 'too good' to talk to them since I was selling a lot of cars. Actually the opposite was true, I was selling a lot of cars and I just didn't have time to stand around and visit with them anymore.

You'll face this same dilemma, too, so I'll say it again – you'll have to make a *choice* and decide whether you're going to work to make a living for you and your family, or to hang around all day with friends. Keep in mind, if the people at work are really friends, they'll totally support your new efforts to improve and grow. If they aren't supportive, they weren't real friends in the first place.

Just go to work – to work!

CHAPTER 16

Your Big Choice

Everything we've talked about in this book will help you get to that $100,000 income level – and even higher. But to make the changes to reach those levels, you're faced with the toughest choice of all.

Reading this book is the easy part. The challenge is to do what we're talking about in here. That means you have to develop your skills, organize your day and start building your business. This is where those 'choices' we've been talking about get even tougher because it means you'll have to make changes and trade your old habits and beliefs for new, more successful ones.

'Insanity'... is doing the same thing over and
over again, expecting a different result each time.
That means to grow – you have to change.

The BIG Choice

Those 'trades' you need to make to become a high achiever in sales are some of the key reasons people don't follow through on their goals, and why they never hit the big time in sales or anything else. The trades we're talking about sound like they're too hard and most people just aren't willing to do the work it takes to hit their goals.

The top 20% are willing to go the extra mile compared to the 80%'ers, and they do get their rewards. However, we all know that it's really the very top 3% who set goals the right way, and earn 10 times as much money as the average person who doesn't set goals.

Those trades you have to make to become a professional in sales and earn professional wages are worth it, though. Shouldn't trading-in some of that TV time really be no problem? Most people watch TV they don't even like, and spend more time watching TV than they spend working. Make a smart trade – turn the TV off.

You may have to trade-in a few friends (or people you thought were friends) when you go to work to work. That's OK though, because isn't your loyalty to your family who depends on you – and not to a bunch of guys you work with who just want to waste your day?

You'll definitely have to spend some money to grow and improve. If you came off a farm like I did and think wearing that purple ski jacket with the stuffing sticking out screams 'I'm a pro', you may have missed a few points I covered. You'll need to look, act and sound like a pro, and you only get one shot at a great 1st impression with each customer – it's a trade off again, so buy a suit.

You'll have to attend a class or two, get a computer or Smartphone, the planners and other tools you need to get better organized (and more productive). That's a good trade, because training pays you back $30 again and again for every $1 you invest.

Find a trusted partner (another good salesperson) and split deals instead of trying to be the hero on every deal. That costs you sales and you never get a day off. Paul and I worked together, sold 30+ each and split dozens of deals every month, *and took our time off.*

Changing what you say to customers may be a harder trade you have to make. I used to think, "Hey, how's it going – how can I help you guys?" was a friendly way to greet people. If you try it a few times, you'll realize 72% of the people respond to that friendly greeting with, "We're just looking." That's just *a reflex response,* but now you have your *first buying objection.* Or on incoming calls – we talk about not 'educating' the customer on the phone and avoiding price (so you get a chance to see them on the lot). I know you're hoping this will actually work, but go ahead and toss out price a few more times, blow a few more commissions, and you'll find that 96% of those customers say, "Thank you very much," and buy down the street after they shop your price. Don't fight it – trade-in your old words and learn to bypass price and double your income.

But the most important thing I hope you realize at this point is that your potential in this business is unlimited.

If you've been doing this awhile, I know there's an 80% chance you've put in tons of hours trying to sell more cars. I know it's probably been a struggle, and that it's been tough to even make a living some months. And I know old habits are hard to break.

"I am who I am – and I can change."

But one thing I've learned is that people can change, and that you can do anything you set your mind to. I know you can do it, because I wrote that statement above in one of my old 3-ring binders when I first started learning more and seeing my potential. When I wrote that, I lived in a cheap apartment, had no job and was totally broke.

I've experienced the changes I'm asking you to make, and I've met so many other people who are just totally blown away at how easy, fun, rewarding and stable a career as a professional in sales in the car business can be – once they've had the proper training. If I've done my job, I've talked you into believing you can become a professional, too.

Congratulations again on your desire to 'be all you can be' in sales. It is my pleasure to work with you and I hope Joe Verde Sales & Management Training, Inc., becomes your training partner for life!

Have a great career!

~~The End~~

This is not the end – it's just the opposite.

It's the beginning of your new life in sales as a

High Achiever Who Earns Over $100,000, Every Year!

We'll see you in class soon,

"From 8 to 38.5!"

"When I first started selling cars my average was 8 per month. In the last two years I have attended two Joe Verde Workshops, I use his Monthly Planning Guides daily and his VSA® (software) to manage my customers. Now my 90 day average is 38.5!

I do well because I eat, live and breathe Joe Verde methods, training and processes. I am proof it works and I can honestly say I do not know where I would be without Joe!"

> *– Trent, Salesperson, Utah*

Joe Verde
Sales Training Workshops

Special Alumni Rates For Previous Attendees! Call Now!

2-Day Professional Selling Skills Workshop

How To Sell A Car And Close The Sale Today!

2 powerful days on the skills salespeople need to succeed. This Interactive Training Workshop has been developed just for you to handle the changes in today's new market.

2-Day Closing And Negotiating Interactive Workshop

Process + Skills = More Sales In Today's Market!

To close more sales with maximum gross profit you need consistent closing and negotiating skills. Learn how to present, close and overcome objections in a 3-Pass Negotiation Process.

2-Day Business Development Workshop

Turn Your Phone And Internet Leads Into Deliveries Now!

Your telephone's ringing and you're missing sales if you don't have the skills and a plan to handle your calls. Turn your incoming leads into appointments that show, and learn to prospect, follow-up and manage the leads you get now.

"I sold 5 cars my first day after your class."

"Joe, I was averaging 10 cars a month, went to your class and then everything came together. I applied what I learned in class and I sold 5 cars and earned $4,204 my first day back at work. That's what I would normally make in a month. I will never be able to thank your training staff enough."

– Tim, Ford Salesperson, Canada

Joe Verde Workshops Across North America

This is a typical snapshot of our class locations.
You can always find a workshop that fits your schedule.

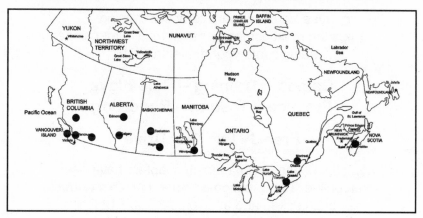

For more information call 800-445-6217

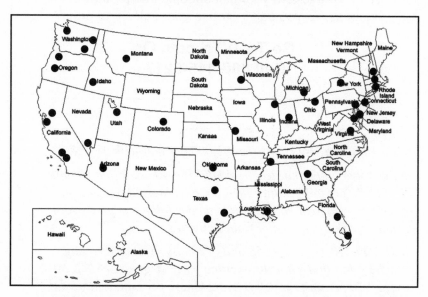

There are dozens of reasons to justify why you can't attend
class and they all sound good. But taking charge of your career
and earning over $100,000 every year sounds even better.

"We increased our gross $1,000 per unit with JVTN®!"

"October 2009, our dealership did $58,403 and sold 30 units ($1,946 per unit). Since then, we have started training on JVTN® and focused a lot more on our follow-up processes along with tracking all of our activities.

October 2010, we sold 58 units (2 units short of doubling sales), but that's not the exciting part, we grossed $172,280 ($2,970 per unit) which is $1,024 more per unit, and we did it with almost 90% being repeat and referral customers. So thanks Joe, your processes work and we are the proof!"

– Skip, General Manager, VW, Canada

Joe Verde
Management Training Workshops

2-Day Team Leadership: Manage Salespeople To Double Net

How to manage your salespeople in today's market!

Improve your 7 core management skills that determine who you hire, how you manage and your ability to control unit sales and gross profit. Develop these skills and double your net profit!

2-Day Negotiating & Desking Deals In Today's Market

Work every deal for maximum gross and great CSI!

Learn this simple, customer friendly 3-Pass Negotiation Process and let us teach your salespeople to set your deals up correctly and you'll easily increase your sales 20% and your gross 40%. Get your salespeople and managers on the same page, now!

3-Day Train Your Trainer & One-On-One Coaching Workshop

Turn your managers into effective trainers and coaches!

That old excuse, "They should learn on their own," just doesn't work in today's tougher market. It's simple, learn to train and coach your salespeople, and sales and profits go up. Sign up today!

"From 60 to 117 units & grosses up $1,100 per unit."

"Before training with the Joe Verde Group our dealership was averaging 60 new units a month. We knew we needed to make changes and attended Joe's 2 Day Manager Workshop. We came back ready to commit to selling Joe's way.

Since attending, we implemented JVTN® and sent the majority of our sales staff to Joe's 2 Day Sales Workshop. Our dealership sold 117 new cars last month and our front end gross has increased by $1,100 per unit. We could not have done it without Joe and his support staff!"

– GSM-Chrysler, Jeep, Dodge, Oklahoma

Joe Verde Resources
Mentioned In This Book*

Get This Book FREE
For Your Salespeople Or Friends!

Go to JoeVerde.com/freebook2 and
Download your FREE PDF copy of this book
Or purchase printed copies in 5-packs for $25
Includes shipping in the U.S.

Are You Ready To
"Go To Work To Work"?

Listen to this audio on your way to work or anytime you want
to get yourself more motivated to sell more cars every day!
Go To JoeVerde.com/GTWTW
Download Your FREE MP3

Two Ways To Get Better Organized,
Set Goals And Sell More Cars!

#1 – FREE Monthly Planning Guide + FREE Sample
Get a FREE Monthly Planning Guide and a FREE Sample MPG
Call or send $3 for shipping

#2 – How To Use Your Monthly Planning Guide – Online
Watch Joe's FREE online video:
"How Can I Set Better Goals & Manage My Selling Day?"
Go to JVTN.com/salesmpg

Joe's Monthly Sales Newsletter
"Selling Cars Today"

You need new and updated information and
Joe's easy to read, monthly newsletters are your answer.
Each month, they're filled with winning sales strategies and
sales tips guaranteed to keep you focused, ready for success
and moving toward your $100,000+ a year sales goal!

Go to JoeVerde.com/SNL to download a FREE PDF

* All special offers are subject to change without notice.

"From 14 to 22 units with JVTN®"

"I've sold cars for 6 years now and was averaging 14 units a month. My dealership got the Joe Verde Online Training® along with Joe's Book 'How to Sell a Car Today'.

For one month I trained, practiced and applied what I learned out on the lot daily and sold 22 units. I have had other sales training and I must say, nothing comes close to the Joe Verde way!"

– Keith, Salesperson, Hyundai, ON

Earn over $100,000 every year!
If you'll believe it – you can achieve it.

Beware of the imposter who will promise they can teach you everything I've just covered.

Don't waste your time – save your money. If they really could, they would have written this book.

– Joe Verde